MOBSTERS AND THUGS

QUOTES FROM THE UNDERWORLD

PROSE SERIES 50

Canadä

Guernica Editions Inc. acknowledges support of The Canada
Council for the Arts.
Guernica Editions Inc. acknowledges support from
the Ontario Arts Council.
Guernica Editions Inc. acknowledges the financial support of the
Government of Canada through the Book Publishing Industry
Development Program (BPIDP).

Olindo Romeo Chiocca

Mobsters and Thugs

Quotes from the Underworld

Guernica

Toronto·Buffalo·Lancaster (U.K.)

2000

Antonio D'Alfonso, editor
Guernica Editions Inc.
P.O. Box 117, Station P, Toronto (ON), Canada M5S 2S6
2250 Military Road, Tonawanda, N.Y. 14150-6000 U.S.A.
Gazelle, Falcon House, Queen Square, Lancaster LA1 1RN U.K.

Printed in Canada.

Legal Deposit — First Quarter
National Library of Canada
Library of Congress Catalog Card Number: 00-100948

Canadian Cataloguing in Publication Data
Chiocca, Olindo Romeo
Mobsters and thugs : quotes from the underworld
(Prose series ; 50)
ISBN 1-55071-104-0
1. Gangsters – Quotations. I. Titles. II. Series.
PN6048.C7C48   2000   364.1   C00-900164-6

There is No Mafia

"There is no Mafia."

This was the callow philosophy of J. Edgar Hoover, FBI director from 1924-1972. Under Hoover's reign as America's leading lawman, a bunch of loose knit hoodlums scattered over America were able to coalesce into a powerful nationally affiliated crime organization of major economical and sociological impact, generating over $100 billion in revenue. Not until an accidental uncovering of a major underworld conference at Apalachin New York in 1957, where over sixty leading mob figures were attending did Hoover creep into action, about forty years too late. According to Carl Sifakis in *The Mafia Encyclopedia,* "J. Edgar Hoover was the best FBI director organized crime could ever have wanted...Without a man like Hoover heading the FBI it is inconceivable that organized crime and the Mafia could ever have reached the heights of power, wealth and administrative organization."

*

"The existence of a secret organization known as the Mafia has been established beyond doubt."

As early as 1890, a U.S. Grand Jury statement confirmed the existence of the Mafia as an institution for organized crime in America. This statement was based on the meticulous work of Mafia assassinated New

Orleans Chief of Police, David Hennessey. It's incredible that in his forty-eight years as FBI director J. Edgar Hoover was never made aware of this document. Really! What could have he been doing for those forty-eight years?

*

"We're bigger than U.S. Steel."

While Hoover kept himself busy chasing petty crooks he continued to ignore the reality of the Mafia. It was as if he was being pelted by a storm of silver dollars while looking for a dime he dropped somewhere. All the while Meyer Lansky, Lucky Luciano and the rest of the associates were busy running and entrenching the national crime syndicate, a very slick and efficient money making crime organization whose influence, power and revenue is still beyond comprehension. By the time he died at eighty-one years, Lansky, according to Jay Robert Nash in *The Encyclopedia of Organized Crime,* "had lived to see his monstrous creation become the second most powerful force in America after the federal government." At the time of his death, Lansky's fortune was estimated to be worth more than $400 million.

*

"Obviously we have neither the manpower nor the time to waste on such speculative measures… it's a fishing expedition."

Again, Hoover with another one of his quotable gems, occurring when he was requested to assign FBI men to Milton Wessel's special crime investigative task force. The task force was mandated to gather intelligence on organized crime individuals and operations for grand jury proceedings (1958).

Speculation varies as to why J. Edgar Hoover was reluctant to deal with the Mafia and organized crime. Historian Albert Fried argued that Hoover believed that organized crime "constituted no immediate danger to established order," while Hoover biographer Hank Messick stated that "John Edgar Hoover has received support, as well as more tangible rewards, from right-wing businessmen who, in turn, have dealt directly and indirectly with organized crime figures who have not been disturbed by John Edgar Hoover." But the general belief is that the unsophisticated Hoover was intimidated by the Mafia and justified his inaction by claiming that the Mafia didn't exist.

*

"The FBI has much more important functions to accomplish than arresting gamblers all over the country."

What those functions were is still unclear. Being an avid player of the horses, Hoover perhaps couldn't see that, with prohibition gone, the money the mob earned from its gambling operations was being used to

a. finance its growth and political influence in America;
b. consolidate its power base;
c. finance its entrenchment in the global drug trade;
d. develop sophisticated methods to launder money;
e. fix the horse races so that tips given to Hoover through Frank Costello would be winners;
f. pay the dental bills of poor orphaned children;
g. all of the above;

h. a and b, but not g or f.

Edgar may have looked sharp in his snappy suits with his second in command, one step behind yes-man, Clyde Tolson tagging along, but as soon as he opened his mouth and said anything... Hoover's status started to be questioned.

*

"The business of the country is business."

That was the muffled conviction of U.S. president Warren Harding (1921-1923) during prohibition. Harding, obviously not a member of the Women's Temperance Movement himself, had complete contempt for the Volstead Act and the tea totallers who advocated it. He enjoyed his own personal cocktail lounge right in the White House, serving booze supplied by the nation's official "First Bootlegger" Elias Mortimer, to valued guests. Even though Harding disagreed with the 18th Amendment he did nothing about it, and it wasn't until 1933 when Franklin Delano Roosevelt and his Democrats took over that the Act was repealed.

*

"I'm not talking about Italians, I'm talking about criminals."

While testifying to the Senate Permanent Investigations Subcommittee in 1963, Joseph Valachi did his best to dispel the myth that all Italians were part of the Mafia. The myth was probably born out of the New York and Chicago ghettos, where the Italian gangsters methodically took control from the Jews and the Irish. The 1951 televised Kefauver hearings which interviewed over 600 "witnesses" started to fuel the glamorous myth of the Mafia. By 1972, the motion picture release of Mario Puzo's *The Godfather* gave the sensation hungry American people what they were looking for: the confirmation that the Mafia was integral to the culture and cuisine of the Italian people.

*

"While I'm sitting on the bench I have my right hand and my left hand."

Martin T. Manton was a corrupt U.S. federal judge who brashly took bribes with both hands. Over a ten year period, Manton produced over 600 legal opinions, most of them in favour of Mafia associates who greased those palms. By 1939, Manton's suborn ways were uncovered and he was brought to trial. In trying to dodge the law in his habitually oily way he stated, "From a broad viewpoint, it serves no public policy for a high judicial officer to be convicted of a judicial crime. It tends to destroy the confidence of the people in courts." The presiding judge scoffed and sentenced the "underhanded" Manton to two years in jail. In 1946, Manton died in complete humiliation.

*

"There is no law against carrying cases... case dismissed."

This decision was handed down by another underworld influenced judge in a case where a witness had testified to seeing about 100 cases of bootleg liquor being carried by the boat in question. This judge's blatant twisting of the law was just another of the endless examples where corrupt judges on the "crime roll" made sure that bootleg operations continued to function unobstructed (1920-30s).

*

"We vote whatever is the best way to make money. If it's going to be one of these guys who is going to be on the reform kick all the time, we'll all band together and vote against him. I'm a registered Democrat but I voted for Nixon in 1968, and I bet the mob really turns out for Nixon in 1972."

The importance of having powerful people in high places did not slip Vinnie Teresa. Nixon, a known friend of crime czar Meyer Lansky, had associated with Bugsy Siegel and Mickey Cohen, who by sheer coincidence donated $26,000 to Nixon's Congressional campaign. Below is a brief list of how Nixon helped return favours to some of his "supporters."

1. Gyp DeCarlo, New Jersey mafia boss was granted a full pardon by Nixon in 1972, one and a half years into a twelve year extortion sentence, on the basis of De-Carlo's "poor health." Apparently Nixon had a soft spot for sick extortionists.

2. Jimmy Hoffa was granted a full pardon in 1971 by Nixon on the condition that he stay out of union activities for ten years. Hoffa had been convicted of bribing a juror in an extortion trial which resulted in a hung jury, and later of misusing $1.7 million of union money. Once released, Hoffa got right back into the action and tried to get his old job back. Nixon? He

didn't apply for that or any posh union job after finding himself unemployed in 1974.

*

"Now why, you may ask, does the government have a right to make you pay taxes? Well, it's a fair question. The answer to that question, Woody, is that you pay taxes for the right to live and work and make money at a legit business. Does that make sense? Well, it's the exact same situation. You did a crooked job in Brooklyn. You worked hard and you earned a lot of money. Now you got to pay your taxes on it just like in the straight world. Because we let you do it. We're the government. That's why I say we're always in the picture."

Carmine "The Snake" Persico was trying to explain to an entrepreneurial crook named Woody the economic theories behind the Profaci "tax" collection system. Woody had ripped off May's Department Store for about half a million dollars and, having done all the work, felt that he should be exempt from the crushing Profaci Tax, or at least qualify for a few tax deductions. Carmine disagreed and tried to explain to him as politely as possible that if he didn't pay the Profaci tax pronto, the IRS (Internal Rubout Service) would pay him a final "audit."

Top Ten Hits
(As selected by KillBoard Magazine)

Eliminating the competition in the cut-throat under-world business arena wasn't accomplished through price wars by slashing the rates on the protection and extortion rackets or by allowing insurance drug plans to pay for narcotics. It also wasn't accomplished by allowing "Johns" the right to two subsidized visits a month to their favorite hooker just because they had a doctor's note indicating undue career or domestic duress. Eliminating the competition literally meant "removing" the competition from the face of the earth through the use of garlic tipped bullets, shotguns, ice-picks, meat-hooks, cattle prods, automatic weapons, bombs... Listed below are the top ten examples, plus a couple of bonus quotes, which I think represent some of the best quips and descriptions of gangland "rub-outs" from the mouths of the very perpetrators themselves.

10

"Seven out of ten times, when we hit a guy, we're wrong... but the other three times we hit, we make up for it."

Sam "Momo" Giancana, a high ranking West Side Chicago crime boss knew that his gang's murder effectiveness ratio (MER) was too low. But hopefully for Momo his ex-colleagues worked on the numbers a little better than he did before they decided to make him statistically insignificant. Sammy was shot in the head seven times from behind while cooking himself some sausages and hot peppers late one night in the comfort of his own home (June 19, 1975).

9

"He ain't done yet."

After having pumped a handful of slugs into bailiff Paul A. Labriola in broad daylight, the terminally necrotic Chicago bootlegger Angelo Genna noticed that his victim was still twitching. Being a thoroughly humane murderer, he straddled the prone Labriola and fired three shots directly into Labriola's head, obliterating the face and scattering his skull all over the pavement. Subsequently, Labriola stopped twitching (March 8, 1921).

8

"I can't stand squealers."

The degenerate and morally bankrupt Albert Anastasia must have been having a real bad day when he made this remark. While watching the TV news that day Albert saw eyewitness Arnold Shuster point out bank robber Willie Sutton (who had no connections with Albert) to the police. This enraged Albert so much that Albert had Arnold tracked down and killed by his Murder Inc. goons (1952).

7

"I'll see you and bump you!"

After luring mobster Rocco Morganti into a card game, accomplished assassin Kid Twist Reles dealt Rocco a magnificent hand of cards. Rocco, now ready to win large, had anted up big time. Reles, already certain of who the loser was going to be, called the bets by pulling out his gun and shooting Morganti point blank in the snout, killing him instantly... Years later, when Kid Twist turned informant he particularly enjoyed recounting this tale to the New York District Attorney, who apparently got quite a few laughs out of it (1930).

6

"I ain't smilin' on either side of my face!"

One of Hell's Kitchen's more sensitive murderers was Happy Jack Mulraney. Jack had a quirky facial defect where it forced him to smile "crooked-like." One day he was asked by his best friend Paddy the Priest why he smiled on only one side of his face. Happy Jack, who perhaps lost a few bucks at the track that day, was so easily offended that he put his gun to Paddy's forehead, made this remark, and then blew Paddy's brains out (1900s).

5

"Even if it takes all day, I tail him and find the right spot... It was an easy pop. I take the ax and sink it in the guy's head. It's the kind of thing that will make a lot of holler. Dames and guys will

make a run out of there. I just run with them and the getaway is a cinch. This is natural."

Harry "Pittsburgh Phil" Strauss, dedicated member of Murder Incorporated and Rhodes Scholar in the art of murder, took the executing of his tasks seriously. Strauss meticulously planned his hits and often encouraged discussion groups and assassin circles with his associates to keep up with new ideas and industry related technologies that were available to help make business easier, cleaner and more profitable. Here Strauss exchanges notes on theatre-murder tactics with murder colleague Kid Twist Reles (1930s).

4

"Take that! No horse can kill a pal of mine and get away with it!"

Two Gun Alterie was a brazen O'Bannion gunman who had a compulsive obsessive behaviour for killing. When his bootlegging buddy Samuel J. "Nails" Morton was kicked to death by a horse, Alterie was so upset that he went back to the rental stable, punched the horse in the snout and then executed the beast using both of his .38 revolvers. Later, he called the owner and told him, "We taught that damn horse of yours a lesson. If you want the saddle, go and git it" (1923).

3

"He came out of his office with his wife. He kissed her in front of the office and I was worried I couldn't get a shot. But he turned and went for the corner. She was standing there watching when I got

him. I don't think I missed once. You could see the dust coming off his coat when the bullets hit."

"Buster from Chicago" was an expert marksman and feared assassin. On this hit, which was recounted by Joseph Valachi, Buster made every effort to only kill James Catania, alias Joe Baker and not to waste any bullets on Catania's wife. As for the dusty coat, perhaps if Joe had been smart enough to go to the cleaner's that day he may have avoided getting "dusted" (1920s).

2

"Jackson was hung up on that meat hook. He was so fucking heavy he bent it. He was on that thing three days before he croaked. He was floppin' around on the hook, Jackie. We tossed water on him to give the prod a better charge, and he's screamin'..."

Fiore Buccieri and James Torello, soldiers of Sam "Momo" Giancana, were reminiscing the good old days of slow torture and murder with their friend Jackie while they were being taped by the FBI. The two, with the help of a couple of others shot the loan-shark Willie in the knee, bound him and then hoisted the 350 lb. man on to a meat hook. They then beat him with a baseball bat, stabbed him with ice picks and scorched him with blow torches. Thinking that that wasn't enough pain, they occasionally stuck an electric cattle prod up his ass. Later, Buccieri got lots of laughs from those in attendance, especially when he handed out candid photos he had taken at the scene (August 1961).

1

"Sometimes guys really suffer, you know? I once saw a guy get shot right up the ass. Man, did he suffer."

Mob executions often vary in technique, duration and in the level of pain inflicted. Mafia mythology has many believe that the method used to eliminate a person is often a reflection of the respect for that individual. In this case, the Profaci gunman must have witnessed a "buckwheat's" execution, where an example is being made of the victim by inflicting pain for a prolonged period.

0

"I kill only bad people."

Charles Birger was a shameless, murdering bootlegger from Williamson County Illinois, he walked around town packing double pistols while being surrounded by a dozen armed goons for protection. One day his two daughters returned from school and were upset about being teased by their classmates about Birger's line of work. When they asked him if he really was the cold blooded killer all the kids said he was, Birger replied by justifying his murderous practices on a moral ground (1920s).

Bonus Hit

"They always piss. Sometimes they shit. Count yourself lucky."

When Jimmy "The Weasel" Fratianno and a couple of his henchmen finished strangling Frankie Niccoli in Jimmy's swank home, Jimmy became upset because, upon death, the victim pissed all over his new rug. Jimmy probably lightened up after one of his more experienced goons explained that the mess could have been a lot uglier and stinkier.

"Most gentile Mr. Silvani, you will be so good as to send me $2,000 if your life is dear to you. So I beg you warmly to put on your door (the moolah) within four days. But, if not, I swear this week's time not even the dust of your family will exist. With regards, believe me to be your friend."

This warm and polite sounding extortion note, common at the turn of the century, was written by prolific Chicago Black Hander Joseph Genite. Neighbourhoods throughout the U.S.A. were terrorized by these spineless murderers who continually preyed on the vulnerability of innocent families which for a time was an accepted part of life. But, by the early 1920s, the stench of the black handers began to fade with the commencement of prohibition, as illegal liquor soon became the real money maker, lifting these relatively small time goons into criminal superstars (1800-1920).

*

"It don't make much difference how cold the air is now. I will be out of the air soon."

Just prior to being hung for murder in Baltimore, Henry Gambrill was offered a warm capote by the attending sheriff. The sheriff was a sensitive man who was concerned that Gambrill might catch the flu or a sore throat in the cold air. Gambrill declined, seeing

worse things than the crisp air affecting his gullet
(1859).

*

*"You're arresting me, huh? I cut some ice in this
town! I made half the big politicians of New York."*

Edward "Monk" Eastman who was one of the first
crime bosses of New York City, was as strong as a bull
and just as smart. Sometime in 1903, while Eastman was
being arrested for assault, he divulged his sources of
influence. The press got a hold of the story and the news
of his political wrangling and influence was quickly all
over town. Even though he was successfully defended by
state senator and Tammany Hall man Thomas Grady
(Tammany Hall was the executive committee of the New
York Democratic Party which was controlled by the Irish
Immigrants by the 1830s and converted into a potent
and often corrupt political machine that guided politics,
vice and gambling for decades), his support from the
Tammany bosses quickly melted away. By 1904, Eastman was sent to Sing Sing for ten years on charges that
would have easily been dismissed years earlier.

The Monk's Actual Thug Services Price List (1898)

Ear Chawed Off	$15.00
Leg or Arm Broken	$19.00
Shot in Leg	$25.00
Stab	$25.00
Doing the Big Job	$100.00 and up

Monk Eastman may actually have had a thread of business acumen running though his skull; he was sort of the

marketing pioneer of his day. Apparently, as the intimidation and mutilation business for the Monk improved, he distributed this price list to his clients, informing them that, although he had expanded his line of services, he was still maintaining his popular cut-throat prices. Sadly, however, the brochure did not indicate if there was an extra charge for cleanup and disposal of the corpse.

*

"I like to beat up a guy every now and then. It keeps me hand in."

Monk Eastman was reflecting on how he attained spiritual enlightenment through "therapeutic" sessions. Once, having just finished a session, he was asked why he had clubbed a seemingly innocent pedestrian unconscious. Eastman pulled out his knife, notched his club and said, "I just wanted to make it an even fifty" (1900s).

*

"It ain't nothin', officer. Rosie here ain't as dainty as she could be — made a pig of herself. I tol' her not to wipe her nose wit da tablecloth. Manners is important! Anyway I only give her a little poke, just enough to put a shanty on her glimmer. But I always takes off me knucks first."

The ham fisted Monk was answering to the police after one of his "flatbacks," Rosie, complained of being brutally beaten by the Monk. Always a man of etiquette, the beastly Monk knew never to hit a girl with his brass knuckles on (1900s).

*

"I'll take care of dem myself."

When questioned by police, The Monk refused to divulge the identities of the men who had beaten and shot him twice. Once released from hospital, he kept his word and killed the leader of the gang responsible by crushing his skull and most of his other bones (1901).

*

"He was the best man they ever had at the polls."

A Manhattan detective in the early 1900s recognized the "political" influence that Eastman had over New York voters. During the early 1900s, the Monk, along with his herd of Cro-Magnon goons used force and intimidation to convince voters to elect Tammany Hall flunkies. More a man of action than words, the only "survey poll" that the corrugated brow Eastman understood how to use was the one he held in his hand and mobilized to clobber people over the head with.

*

"Oh a lot of little wars around New York."

When Eastman was being examined for WW I service, he proudly explained to the doctor why his body was scarred with numerous bullet and knife wounds. While serving on the hellish Western Front, the bloodthirsty Eastman found himself at home amongst the human carnage, earning medal after medal for his enthusiasm in killing. Of course Eastman survived the war, but he could not survive his return to the gang-lands of New York City. On December 26, 1920, the body of Eastman was found disguised by bullet holes in front of the Bluebird Café. Despite his criminal record the gangland killer was given a full military funeral with honours for his wartime heroics.

*

"De lower east side ain't gonna be run by no wop or no mick."

The proud, yet somewhat illiterate Jewish gang leader Max "Kid Twist" Zwerback had little tolerance for other racial minorities in his New York territory, especially the cross-cultural racketeer Paul Kelly. Kelly, born Paulo Vaccarelli, was an Italian who took on an Irish name, thus being doubly insulted by Max's scurrilous remarks. So on May 14, 1908, while Max was being distracted by the lures of singer Carroll Terry, more than a dozen of Kelly's goons surrounded him. Quickly, "Louie the Lump" Pioggi opened fire and struck Max in the head and heart, killing him before he could utter any more racial slurs.

*

"What's eleven months? I could do that standin' on me head."

When The Lump was being sentenced to just eleven months for killing the powerful crime boss Zwerback, Louie knew that he literally had gotten away with murder. Louie was being backed by Paul Kelly, who bankrolled the necessary corrupt officials to get him off easy. With Max dead, Kelly picked up the lucrative rackets while Louie got "racked." According to unreliable sources, Louie's mind didn't get any sharper after standin' on 'is 'ed.

*

"Let that learn you not to talk so much."

Joe "The Greaser" Rosenzweig may have had a dull sense of grammar, but he carried a sharp pair of shears. When Al Jewback, an over-rated lieutenant in the Pinchy Paul gang, threatened to squeal to authorities after being clubbed by Rosenzweig's thugs, Joe cornered Al and snipped off a piece of his tongue. Al was left speechless (New York, 1910).

*

"The conduct of the police in this case was shameful. They discharged the defendant in the face of all the facts. It shows an absence of honesty and good faith on the part of the police. It was not until you had committed another assault that they were shamed into making an arrest. You should have been convicted of highway robbery. Instead you were convicted of assault only."

In the early 1900s, the application of law in New York City was constantly being dictated by the corrupt political administration of Tammany Hall. In or about 1904, when Tammany Hall patsy and Manhattan crime boss Paul Kelly was arrested for beating and robbing a man, the police were given orders by Tammany Hall big wig Tim Sullivan to change the charges. The resulting term was nine months instead of a potential twenty years, which the incensed Judge Recorder Goff found ludicrous but was powerless to change.

*

"I'm the boss." Gunfire. "Now I'm the boss."

Timmy Quilty and William "Wild Bill" Lovett, two Irish mobsters in the White Hand Gang of New York, agreed that rolling a seven on the dice would determine the new boss of New York's waterfront. When Timmy rolled the lucky seven on his first roll and exclaimed victory, Lovett, the chronic sore loser, pulled out his gun and deposited a few slugs in Timmy's head to reverse the decision (1919).

"This whole town is wide open."

This was the political philosophy of "Big Bill" Hale Thompson, mayor of Chicago from 1915-1923 and 1927-1931. Big Bill may have been one of the most overtly corrupt politicians in American history. He was a narcissistic elected gangster who operated for his own personal and financial gain under the shield of elected office. He caused untold damage to the city and to the lives and livelihood of countless Chicago citizens. As mayor of Chicago, Big Bill was paid fantastic sums from bootlegging rivals Al Capone and Dion O'Bannion for the freedom to run their bootlegging fiefdoms in the city. In addition to the cash, Al and Dion used their army of goons to ensure that Hale was repeatedly elected. The tactics used during elections included ballot box stuffing, strong arming voters, casting multiple ballots, fraud and killing opposing candidates and dissenters.

*

"This will mean millions for us Uncle Jim. People will have nothing to drink. We'll provide the beer, the liquor. What we can't get from Canada, we'll make for ourselves."

Just before the Volstead Act (prohibition, 1920-1933) was enacted on January 16, 1920, John Torrio practically begged his uncle, the early Chicago crime boss Big Jim Colosimo, to use his political muscle to expand into the bootlegging business. Torrio realized that booze was an appropriate addition to his prostitution and gambling rackets and that it would bring in huge sums of money. But Big Jim had become an apathetic and obese crime boss happy to live with the status quo and his new arm-piece wife, singer Dale Winter. Deciding that a more modern approach to business management was needed, Torrio had his uncle murdered by Al Capone. Within five years of the enactment of the Volstead Act, John Torrio was pulling in over $50 million a year of tax free income.

*

"Big Jim and me were like brothers."

A misty eyed John Torrio was longingly recalling sweet moments with his uncle Jim Colosimo after being questioned by police about his uncle's murder. On May 11, 1920, Al Capone put a bullet through Colosimo's head; when Al was questioned, he commented, "Mr. Colosimo and me both loved the opera. He was a grand guy."

*

"There are millions in booze, plenty for everyone. All we gotta do is respect the other guy's area and we'll make money."

The immense potential value of the Volstead Act did not slip by the astute, criminal mind of John Torrio. Torrio, who had just killed off his uncle Big Jim Colosimo, was ready to negotiate liquor distribution territories with rival Dion O'Bannion. The end resulted in Chicago being split mainly into two areas of control (with other minor factions included): the North Side for O'Bannion and his gang; the South Side for the Torrio-Capone gang (1920).

*

His head got away from his hat.

Al Capone was known for his proficient use of a baseball bat when "brainless" associates got out of hand (1920s).

*

Me and Hymie are waiting for the manager. You see, we heard about what good pay these telegraphers get and we decided that we wanted to sign on... You got to get up early to beat the other fella to the opportunities.

Although the nostalgic Dion O'Bannion had millions of dollars coming in yearly from his North Side liquor rackets, he occasionally enjoyed the small heists just for old time's sake. On this occasion, O'Bannion and cohort Hymie Weiss were caught robbing a postal telegraph office safe in the early morning by a policeman. When the dapper thugs explained what they were doing, the officer just stared in disbelief and took them to the precinct. Within an hour of arrival, the two were released (1922).

*

"Now the bum's headed back to New York where he belongs."

When the loyal Dion O'Bannion henchman Samuel "Nails" Morton discovered that the rival Genna Brother's gang had hired New York gun man Frank Constanza to eliminate Dion, Nails was somewhat discombobulated. So, to get himself into a better mood, he ferreted out Constanza and killed him in a close gun battle, then with the help of close buddy Louis Alterie heaved the corpse onto a New York bound boxcar and they waved him good-bye (1922-3).

*

"Capone is a lowlife, and he's got a disease he can't get rid of, everybody knows it."

Dion O'Bannion, Capone's arch enemy and chief antagonist, had few complimentary things to say of the syphilitic Al Capone. Is it any wonder that after what Dion said, the sensitive Capone had O'Bannion filled with lead? (1920s.)

*

"I'm gonna retire, Johnny. The rackets are wearing me out. The Gennas are invading my territory and the bodies are piling up... No more guns, no more street fights."

With death, carnage and piles of stiff carcasses a constant obstacle course on Chicago's streets, Dion

O'Bannion tried to convince rival bootlegger Johnny Torrio that he was going through a mid-life crisis. He claimed he was ready for a career change and was willing to sell his North Side brewery if both sides could come to an agreement. An interested Torrio paid Dion $500,000 cash (credit was frowned upon), right then and there for the brewery. Within minutes of the transaction, sirens whaled and the sting was complete. Torrio had been set up and the police on O'Bannion's payroll arrested the mobster and shut down the brewery. O'Bannion reveled in victory but was warned by "Hymie" Weiss of Torrio's temper. The cocky O'Bannion responded, "I guess I rubbed that pimp's nose in the mud all right. Hymie... Aw, Hymie, when are you gonna learn? Them gutter rats are dumb. To hell with them Sicilians. I clipped the pimp for $500,000 and then dumped him in the can... Them Sicilians can go to hell." On November 10, 1924, under orders from the "gutter rat," Albert Anselmi, John Scalise and Frankie Yale went in to O'Bannion's flower shop on the guise of picking up a funeral wreath and deposited six slugs into Dion, two in the chest, two in the larynx, and two in the face. He was dead before he hit the ground.

*

"From Al."

This was the touching message Al Capone sent with an outrageously expensive funeral wreath to the bereaved family members of Dion O'Bannion.

*

"Public service is my motto. Ninety-nine percent of the public in Chicago drink and gamble. I've tried to serve them decent liquor and square games. But I'm not appreciated. It's no use. I violate the prohibition law, sure. Who doesn't? The only difference is I take more chances than the man who drinks a cocktail before dinner and a flock of hiballs after it. But he's just as much a violator as I am."

All Al Capone really wanted to be when he grew up was a respectable businessman, but he just couldn't understand that the business school terminology of "eliminating the competition" didn't mean you killed them off.

*

"You never get no back talk from no corpse."

Brother to Al, Frank Capone had a short fuse and negotiated with his gun. During the Chicago primaries of 1924, Frank and his gang were roughing up uncooperative voters when police arrived to calm the situation. But before the cops could identify themselves, Capone, sticking with his criminal beliefs to shoot first and ask questions later, started shooting wildly, but was quickly killed by return fire. For the funeral, Al ordered over $20,000 worth of flowers which filled a endless train of shiny black funeral cars. Post-mortum reports indicated that Frankie had little to say about the flower arrangements.

*

"Aww, go back to your girls, you dago pimp."

"Ragtime" Joe Howard was an old-time Chicago punk and hijacker who figured he was tough enough to mess with Al Capone. In May of 1924, Ragtime roughed up Capone's dexterous accountant Jake "Greasy Thumb" Guzik in Heinie Jacob's saloon. When Al found out his loyal money man was being abused, his mind bent and he immediately rushed over to the saloon where Howard hung out and demanded an explanation. Howard, still feeling quite reckless, gave Al this insulting response. Furiously calm, Al put his gun to Howard's head and waited a few seconds for Ragtime to sweat a bead or two and then unloaded the gun into his head, leaving nothing but a pulpy bloody mess all over the bar. Apparently Heinie grunted disapproval as he sopped up the curds. According to scribes, just prior to beating up Guzik, the drunken Howard had bragged to Jacob, "Them Wop beerboys fold up like an old newspaper after one chop."

*

"If those cowardly rats have any guts, they'll meet me at noon at State and Madison and we'll shoot it out."

The brash Louis Alterie had the nerve to say this to reporters right in the office of Chicago police captain John Stege after Capone's men had executed his boss Dion O'Bannion. This so angered Chicago mayor William E. Dever that he replied: "Are we still abiding by the code of the Dark Ages?" (1924.)

*

"I have no idea who killed Deanie, but I would die smiling if only I had the chance to meet the guys who did… I would get at least two or three of them before they got me… I'd shoot it out with the gang of killers before the sun rose in the morning and some of us, maybe all of us, would be lying on slabs in the undertaker's place."

O'Bannion gunman Louis "Two Gun" Alterie just couldn't keep his mouth shut again and again. Hymie Weiss, the new leader of the O'Bannion gang, kept telling Two Gun to keep his trap shut in public because his gibberish was attracting unnecessary heat and was stifling North Side business. But the thick skulled Alterie didn't get it. Soon after, in 1924, at a popular Chicago nightspot, frequented by thugs and scribes alike, Alterie flaunted both his polished pistols up high and announced, "All twelve bullets in these rods have Capone's initials carved on their noses. And if I don't get him, Bugs, Hymie or Schemer will" (1924). Alterie was permanently silenced in 1935 with the help of a number of Capone sanctioned bullets.

*

"This is for Deanie O'Bannion, you dago bastard."

George "Bugs" Moran was just about to blow the head off of fallen John Torrio in revenge for the murder of O'Bannion. Straddling Torrio with his gun pressed against Johnny's head, Moran squeezed only to have the gun misfire; bad luck undoubtedly due to the racial slurs he threw at Johnny. Pressured from police sirens, Moran took off leaving Torrio alive but soiled (January 24, 1925).

*

"Bullets... tipped with garlic."

After being shot, John Torrio lay wounded in front of his home and was overheard by police mumbling something about pungent bullets and their potential health hazard. During that period, Albert Anselmi and John Scalise, Chicago's most feared gunmen and agents for the Genna Brothers, were the main advocates for rubbing their bullets with garlic. They, along with other killers, believed that the seasoned slugs would result in gangrene and kill their victims if the bullet wounds failed. As Torrio was being rushed to the hospital he yelled to the medics, "Cauterize it! Cauterize it!" thinking this would be some kind of antidote.

*

"Anybody resigns from us resigns feet first."

Louis "Little New York" Campagna was such a devoted bodyguard of Al Capone that any type of treachery, real or perceived was brutally dealt with. In fact, Campagna was so devoted to Capone that in many instances he would sleep right outside Capone's hotel bedroom with an arsenal of weapons in and around his bed, ready to defend Capone to the death. This, in spite of Capone having over fifty accomplished killers stationed throughout the hotel to protect him (1920s).

*

"Damn you, kid copper! Now see what you did, you bastard."

The arrogant and vicious murderer Vincent "The Schemer" Drucci, an O'Bannon associate, was shot four times while trying to take Detective Danny Healy's gun as he was being escorted to the Chicago Criminal Courts Building. When Drucci's oily lawyer Maurice Green saw the punk's blood soaked corpse in the car as it arrived at the courts, he rushed into the office of Chicago's Chief of Detectives William "Old Shoes" Schoemaker and demanded justice. With a smug grin, Old Shoes replied; "We're having a medal made for Healy" (April 4, 1927).

*

"I wouldn't do that to a yellow dog."

Al Capone may have had many character defects, but it was the fierce loyalty to his men that helped him become a successful crime baron. In 1926, Hymie Weiss of the North Siders offered Capone a peace settlement to the bootleg turf wars on the condition that Capone surrender the Dion O'Bannion murderers John Scalise and Albert Anselmi. Capone bitterly refused, indicating that he would never betray his own men. A few years later, these very men betrayed Capone and paid the ultimate price.

*

"We know it was you and some others who knocked off the O'Donnells, Frank. You can tell

Capone this for me. I'm gonna get him if I have to kill everybody in front of him to do it..."

When Al Capone had Walter O'Donnell killed in 1924, it enraged Capone rival Hymie Weiss. Weiss, a brutal gunman, warned Capone's top henchmen Frank McErlane of his intent to mop up the filth on city streets with what was left of Capone's corpse. On January 12, 1925, Weiss, along with Moran and Drucci as the artillery, pelted Capone's car with a plague of bullets that just missed Capone's bald scalp, but injured his driver Sly Barton. A week later, they ambushed and nearly killed Capone's partner John Torrio, running him right out of Chicago. Bodies started piling up and the attacks on Capone continued. After a failed attempt at negotiating peace with Weiss, Capone assembled an all star cast of killers to terminate Weiss, including Frank Nitti, Frank Diamond, Scalise and Anselmi. On October 11, 1926, Weiss and his body guard Paddy Murray were completely consumed by a rain of bullets as they were about to enter the Holy Name Cathedral, probably to confess.

*

"There is enough business for all of us without killing each other like animals in the streets."

Going from bar room bouncer to international crime luminary, Capone may have been one of the first gangsters or businessmen of any kind to use the media so effectively for his own benefit. At this press conference, Capone knew that his battle with the O'Bannion North Siders was taking its toll on lives and public opinion, so his goal was to portray himself as the gallant gangster by extending a hand in peace. On October 21,

1926, Capone negotiated a temporary peace with Moran (leader of the O'Bannion gang with Weiss dead), in order to concentrate his forces on the upcoming mayoralty primary in which his candidate William Hale Thompson was running. When asked by the press about the deal, Capone replied, "They stay on the North Side and I stay in Cicero and if we meet on the street, we say 'Hello' and shake hands. Better, ain't it?" Of course there was never any real peace as the rival gangsters never trusted each other, continuing to mow each other down at every opportunity.

*

"Wipe out that nest of Genna snakes, no matter if it takes forever."

Al Capone wanted all six rival Genna brothers dead, but that was one tough assignment even for Al's top gunman Frank Nitti. The Gennas, who controlled distilling operations in the Near West Side of Chicago, were a brutal lot of ruthless killers who were in constant competition with Capone, as well as O'Bannion's North Side gang. Eventually three of the brothers, Angelo, Mike and Tony were killed by various means and groups, while the other three, Pete, Sam and Jim chickened-out and fled Chicago, returning years later to sell cheese, fish heads, anchovies and olive oil (1920s).

*

"Take that, you son of a bitch."

While being carried out by stretcher after being fatally shot in the neck in a police gun battle, the ungrateful Mike Genna gave a final swift kick upwards breaking the ambulance attendant's jaw and knocking him unconscious (June 13, 1925).

*

"When Judgement Day comes and those graves are open, they'll be hell to pay in this cemetery!"

A Chicago police sergeant noted that by a twist of grim fate, arch rivals Tony Genna and Dion O'Bannion were buried within a few feet of each other in Chicago's Mount Carmel cemetery. The battle for territorial supremacy continues right to this day... don't turn around! (1926.)

*

"You buy a judge by weight, like iron in a junkyard. A justice of the peace or a magistrate can be had for a five-dollar bill. In municipal court he will cost you ten. In the circuit or superior courts he wants fifteen. The state appellate court or the state supreme court is on par with the federal courts. By the time a judge reaches such courts he is middle-aged, thick around the middle, fat between the ears. He's heavy. You can't buy a federal judge for less than a twenty dollar bill."

Jake Greasy Thumb Guzik, who was in charge of Capone's pay-offs, knew the going judicial pay scale in order to keep Capone's criminal machinery well lubricated. Jake was nicknamed Greasy Thumb because of the incredible amount of dirty cash he thumbed out to the slippery politicians and oily legal types (Chicago, 1920-30s).

*

"Get out of town or get killed."

Al Capone warned one of his rival bootleggers "Diamond" Joe Esposito to beat it. Joe, who was encouraged even by his own men to retire to his Illinois pig and weasel farms told them: "I'm not that dumb… Some slug trying to scare me out of town so he can grab my operations." Later that day while taking an evening stroll, Joe, who strutted about in a $50,000 diamond studded belt, was sliced to pieces by over fifty garlic fortified machine gun slugs. The garlic tipped bullets were the trademark of Capone killers Anselmi and Scalise who were never questioned in the murder (March, 1928).

*

"I'm going to shoot some pheasants."

Sam "Golf Bag" Hunt was one of Al Capone's more callous gun-men who enjoyed a couple of rounds of golf now and again after a hard day of killing. Golf Bag often pursued his victims toting a golf bag which was loaded with his machine gun and other irons. One day when a detective stopped the notorious killer on suspicion of a murder that had occurred earlier, Hunt gave this terse reply (1920s).

*

"I don't even know what street Canada in on."

Al Capone made carloads of cash from liquor smuggled into the U.S.A. from Canada during prohibition, but he just couldn't seem to afford to put a map up for his own reference.

*

"I'm gonna send Moran a Valentine he will never forget."

On February 14, 1929, Al Capone sent out a bunch of his best torpedoes disguised as cops to kill the remnants of Bugs Moran's North Side gang. In Moran's headquarters, the "cops" stood six of Moran's unarmed men, including gangster groupie Dr. Reinhardt Schwimmer, up against the wall for "frisking" and then machine gunned them in the back. Problem was, Capone's main target, Moran, was late and missed out on his promised Valentine from Al.

*

"I didn't know those guys."

When the corpses from the St. Valentine's Day Massacre were being toe-tagged at the city morgue, Bug's Moran initially denied knowing his very own men.

*

"Only Capone kills like that."

After the killings, Moran was so horrified and panic stricken that he checked himself into a hospital and hid in bed, taking along two of his own torpedoes for protection. When reporters finally found him and asked who could have executed such a grim deed, Bugs broke the criminal code of silence and gave this now famous reply. That act of human butchery was considered totally unacceptable even in those seditious days of Chicago, it was Capone's biggest mistake and the beginning of his eventual demise. The national outrage it created forced authorities to take real action, putting the IRS on the case. Even the sluggish President Herbert Hoover lifted an eyebrow and shifted a buttocks, demanding that Capone be brought to justice at any cost.

*

"Nobody shot me."

Frank Gusenberg, victim of the St. Valentine's Day Massacre miraculously survived for a short while. Even though he knew his end was near and that he had nothing to lose, Frank would not divulge the names of the gunmen even when he was repeatedly asked to by his childhood buddy and Chicago Police Department Sergeant, Frank Sweeney (1929).

*

"If a policeman detains you, even for a moment against your will, you are not guilty of murder, but

only of manslaughter. If the policeman uses force of arms, you may kill him in self defense and emerge from the law unscathed."

This was part of the argument used by Capone's unscrupulous lawyer Michael J. Ahern to defend John Scalise and Albert Anselmi from the charges of murdering two Chicago police officers. The two were eventually acquitted on an appeal of unwarranted police aggression. Michael Ahern was a sort of legal pioneer in his day, as he began to pave the licentious road on which many lawyers to this day have continued to follow and extend (October, 1925).

*

"Not me, Al, honest to God. Johnnie. It was his idea. His and Joe's. Believe me, Al, I wouldn't…"

Capone men Albert Anselmi, John Scalise and "Hop Toad" Giunta conspired with crime family boss Frankie Rio to kill Capone and take over his Chicago operations. Al caught wind of the treachery and at a party he held in their honour, he ceremoniously smashed their skulls with a baseball bat. Albert was the last to get killed and just before getting clobbered, he was willing to say anything to save his own skin. Days earlier while plotting the murder of Capone, the cocky Scalise was overheard saying, "I'm the big shot now, not Al. It falls to me and Albert" (May 7, 1929).

*

"Nobody puts a price on my head and lives."

Al Capone was incensed that west side rival Joseph
Aiello had put a $50,000 bounty on his head, Al prob-
ably figured he was worth much more than that. Later,
Capone got to yellow Aiello and extracted a promise
from him that he would never return to Chicago. Aiello
did return and for three years Capone kept a wary eye
on him, finally snapping when Aiello ordered over
1,500 Sicilian booze benders to stop producing the alky
that supplied Al's bars. In retaliation, Capone sent over
a dozen button men out onto the streets to greet Aiello,
and on Oct 23, 1930, just as he put his toe out the door,
Aiello was ventilated by a hail storm of lead. During his
autopsy, the coroner pulled out more than fifty slugs,
weighing over half a kilo.

*

*"These gang movies are making a lot of kids want
to be tough guys."*

Early gangster movies such as *Little Caesar, Public
Enemy* and *Scarface* were the first to create the false
image of brash tough guys who wore expensive suits.
These gangsters gained respect through fear and intimidation while never having to grind it out from 9 to 5.
Ben Hecht, who was the screenwriter for *Scarface*, was
accosted one evening by two of Al Capone's thirsty
looking thugs who felt that the movie blasphemed Al,
thus demanding an explanation. The sly Hecht wormed
his way out by explaining that the movie was about
other mobsters, such as Big Jim Colosimo, Dion O'Ban-

nion and Hymie Weiss; he then continued to claw his way to safety by telling the goons that the title *Scarface* was used because, "Al is one of the most famous and fascinating men of our time. If you call the movie *Scarface*, everybody will want to see it, figuring it's about Al. That's part of the racket we call showmanship." With this, the dim goons walked away happy. According to Ralph Salerno and John S. Tompkins in their book *The Crime Confederation*, "The movie *Scarface* was so explicit in its exposure of municipal corruption that the city of Chicago banned it until after World War II."

*

"Nobody's gonna Zuta me."

After his death, the name of Frank Zuta came to represent vengeance, retribution or just plain getting even. Zuta was an outstanding mob accountant who had a bad habit of keeping excellent records on all of the mob's transactions. In 1928, Zuta made the mistake of switching allegiances from Al Capone to the O'Bannion gang; so it came as no surprise to anyone when on August 1st, 1930, Zuta was ground-up by eight gunmen wielding submachine guns, automatic pistols and sawed-off shotguns. After his death, Zuta's meticulous records were discovered and they revealed the extent of the blatant corruption within the government and the filthy bureaucrats who could not escape Zuta's ghoulish vengeance. Those shown to be receiving payoffs included: Chicago alderman Dorsey Crowe, former Judge Emanuel Eller, Judge Joseph W. Schulman and state senator Harry W. Starr, among others. All of these oily legal and greasy political types were able to ooze out of trouble by using shifty legal maneuvers, connections, payoffs and double talk. So, in 1931, when Al Capone found out there was a $50,000 price tag on his bald head, he accorded Zuta the respect he deserved.

*

"We wrecked at least twenty bookies, all of them big operators. We took a fortune from them. The big guy in Chicago was very happy, and I went back to New York with a suitcase full of green."

Gerald "Cheesebox" Callahan was one of the few educated hoods of his time. Graduating from college in electronics and gaining valuable experience while working at the Bell Laboratories, he made a stack of cash without ever having to get involved in the blood end of Al Capone's business. Gerald's job was to set taps into the racing wires of the National News Service which circulated race results directly from the track nationwide to betting parlors, bookie joints and backroom dens. The phone taps allowed Capone to alter or delay the race results so that his stooges could place bets on races already completed, guaranteeing big payoffs and wiping out the bookies (1930s).

*

"I can't help it, Bambino, but I'm going."

These were Two Gun Alterie's last words while being cradled in his wife's arms after being mowed down by the machine gun fire of Capone's men. The irony of the situation was that the ambush method used by Capone's men, where the killers would stake out a promising area from an adjacent apartment or hotel room window for days, was developed by Two Gun himself (July 18, 1935).

*

"Have you gotten rid of that fellow Capone yet? Remember, I want that man Capone in jail."

By 1929, President Herbert Hoover finally woke up and saw his nation falling into a lawless ditch and pressed his law enforcement officials in Washington to nail Capone. The St. Valentine's Day Massacre had revealed the law's impotence and Hoover was looking to score brownie points with the body politic. Unfortunately for Hoover, Capone proved to be quite slippery and wasn't imprisoned until 1932 when he was convicted of income tax evasion. He was sentenced to eleven years in prison and fined a paltry $80,000, an amount he earned daily. Fortunately, Hoover didn't last much longer, he was booted out of office by Franklin Delano Roosevelt in 1933.

*

"Get enough, boys, you won't be seeing me for a long time."

In 1931, the grim legacy of Al Capone started to come to an end. After an endless trudge through reams of paper and secretly gathered information from Capone's trusted business agent Edward J. O'Hare, IRS tax investigator Elmer L. Irey was able to put enough evidence together to convict Capone of income tax evasion. As the flabbergasted Capone left the courtroom sentenced to eleven years in a federal penitentiary, he had only this to say to the quip seeking scribes... But as for O'Hare, his legacy was to end sooner. Just after his cover as an informant was revealed, he was shot to death in his car by unidentified assassins (November 19, 1935).

*

"Hey, lard ass, get back at the end of the line... I know who you are, grease ball. And if you don't get back to the end of that fucking line, I'm gonna know who you were."

Al Capone did not command the respect and fear in Alcatraz prison that he did on the streets of Chicago. While serving time for tax evasion, Capone once tried to butt into line for a prison haircut, but a Texan named James Lucas took exception and grabbed the scissors from the barber and threatened to trim Capone's jugular. Capone meekly went back to the end of the line and waited to trim what few strands remained on his near gleaming dome (1935-36?).

*

"You've lost your job.
You've lost your dough.
Your jewels and handsome houses.
But things could be worse, you know,
You haven't lost your trousers."

"Machine Gun" Jack McGurn, Capone hit-man, bootlegger, and participant in the St. Valentines Day Massacre had a habit of placing a five cent piece in the palm of his murder victims. But on Feb 13, 1936, it was

McGurn's turn, he was shot to death in a bowling alley by Bugs Moran and two of his men, apparently as revenge for McGurn's participation in the St. Valentine's Day massacre. In Machine Gun's palm was found a five cent piece and this poem.

*

"Al is nutty as a fruitcake."

The ever compassionate Greasy Thumb Guzik was the only person on the planet who could say such a disparaging remark about Al Capone and see the sunrise the next day. By 1938, after serving about six years in the can, Capone's untreated syphilis had ravaged his entire body and caused paresis of the brain. He had become an incoherent babbling zombie, yelling execution orders to pillars and washbasins. Capone contracted the deadly disease years earlier by engaging in questionable horizontal activities with his own unhygienic and contaminated whores, prostitutes and sluts. Published but unconfirmed reports speculated that the ruthless Capone was never treated for the disease because of his fear of syringes. On January 25, 1947, Al Capone suffered a hemorrhage to what was left of his doughy brain and died.

*

"I've been shot and missed so often I've a notion to hire out as a professional target. Life with me is just one bullet after another."

Edward "Spike" O'Donnell was in a continuous battle with the Capone gang for the distribution control of bootleg liquor in Chicago's Southwest Side. Constantly dodging bullets and surviving numerous attempts on his life, the pithy gangster came to accept his bullet dodging fate. On September 25, 1925, Frankie McErlane, gunman on loan from Capone ally "Polack" Joe Saltis, unloaded a volley of lead into O'Donnell leaving him for dead in a sticky pool of blood. The buoyant Spike survived, heeded the warning and retired from the business.

*

"Baby, let me say this. I got one eye, and that one eye sees a lot of things that my brain tells me I shouldn't talk about. Because my brain says that, if I do, my one eye might not be seeing anything after a while."

Sammy Davis Jr., along with the other Rat Packers which included Frank Sinatra, Dean Martin, Joey Bishop and Peter Lawford, often performed free as favours to Frank Sinatra's friends such as Sam Giancana. When questioned by federal agents, Sammy knew which audiences he shouldn't be singing to (1950s).

*

"Me?... I steal."

When Momo Giancana, who controlled the Chicago mob from 1957-66 was asked what he did for a living when being interviewed for World War II service, he could only tell the truth. But the army figured otherwise and declared him 4-H, a constitutional psychopath and sent him home. A subsequent police report on

Momo described him as "a snarling, sarcastic ill-tempered, sadistic psychopath." Just what the army said. Years later, after having a few glasses of red wine, Sam told friends of his recruitment incident and commented, "They thought I was crazy. But I wasn't crazy, I was telling the truth."

*

"If Bobby Kennedy wants to talk to me, I'll be glad to talk to him and he knows who to go through."

Sausage loving Mafioso socialite Momo Giancana was so fed up with being tailed by federal agents that he sent them this terse message via his trusted criminal confidante Charles English. According to *The World Encyclopedia of Organized Crime*, the liaison between the White House justice department and the Mafia was crooner Frank Sinatra (1960s).

*

"That man must want something: money, favours, a seat in the Supreme Court. Find out what he wants and get it for him."

In 1943, Paul "The Waiter" Ricca, Chicago crime boss prior to and after Momo, was sentenced to ten years for his role in the extortion attempt of the Hollywood movie industry. While in prison, he gave his cunning lawyer explicit instructions on who needed to be greased in order to get him out of jail quickly. By 1947, Ricca was released, mainly due to the manipulative dealings of Attorney General Tom Clark. The early release caused the Chicago press to go wild with the speculation of Ricca's White House Connections, but regardless of the commotion, Ricca got what he paid for and was now able to continue building the mobs criminal influence in America. Tom Clark? He was later appointed to the Supreme Court by President Harry Truman.

*

"I didn't know then that Sam was the Chicago Godfather. But I did know he was important to Frank because of the way Sinatra acted around him, bowing and scraping and being so deferential."

Hollywood and political socialite Judith Campbell Exner knew slavish behaviour when she saw it. Judith orbited around a variety of social groups and was alleged to have had affairs with Frank Sinatra, Senator and President John F. Kennedy and Chicago mob don Sam Giancana. Exner, who had left Sinatra and was deep in affair with Kennedy was introduced to Giancana by Sinatra. Soon, Exner was being used as a go between for Giancana and Kennedy, where Kennedy requested and obtained Giancana's help to secure key wards in the 1960 West Virginia and Chicago primaries. Many political analysts concluded that Giancana's power of political persuasion in Chicago was a key element in Kennedy's razor thin victory over Richard Nixon.

*

"Listen honey, if it wasn't for me, your boyfriend wouldn't even be in the Whitehouse."

Momo to Judith Campbell Exner on JFK. 'Nuff said.

*

"They were all bum raps. And besides, I had a good lawyer."

Lawrence "Dago" Mangano, a Chicago rackets boss, had been arrested over 200 times during his nefarious career but never served a day in prison. With bags of dirty money available, Mangano was able to attract shifty egghead lawyers who could keep him out of the slammer. The names may have changed but the legal precedents and shifty eyed questionable types remain the same (1920-30s).

*

"I'll pull your eyeballs out. I'll put ice picks in you."

Demented Chicago enforcer, loan-shark and extortionist Sam DeStefano, who killed his own brother when he was ordered to, had a peculiar way of convincing Mob debtors to pay on time. The twisted Sam reveled in his work to such an extent that he would constantly research and think up new and improved ways to inflict excruciating pain on his victims; keeping them alive and in pain as long as possible. One of Sam's favourite methods was to shove his quarry into a phone booth and continually jab an ice pick into their stomach. In one special case, Sam took one of his delinquent clients to a jeweler and bought him a watch inscribed with, "From Sam to Bob." Sam explained the engraving to the shaking stooge thus: "So when they find you in a trunk they'll know I was your friend" (1940s-1960s).

*

"Make him go away."

Paul Ricca, Chicago boss of bosses, was a murderer and extortionist with a cool head. Paul knew when he wanted someone eliminated and he used few words to mandate it.

*

"I've been expecting it. The bastards never forget."

Former Chicago bootlegging beer brewing magnate Roger "The Terrible" Touhy had been out of jail for just twenty-three days after serving a twenty-five year sentence when he was whacked on the doorstep of his sister's home. Touhy, who had been sent to jail on framed-up kidnapping charges, had jokingly frightened Capone associate Murray "The Camel" Humphreys with machine gun fire in 1931. The Camel, who never forgot, never forgave, and twenty-eight years later on December 17, 1959, practically sliced Touhy in half with a number of shotgun blasts.

*

"I'll just live quietly in the country, that's all."

Minutes after making this wish known to reporters after leaving Will County Courthouse, William Dauber, a high powered assassin and Chicago crime boss was gunned down along with his wife while driving along a peaceful tree lined country road (July 1980).

*

"Shaddup or I'll bust ya in da teets."

This was the favorite line used by Chicago loan-shark and syndicate leader Samuel 'teets' Battaglia whenever anyone challenged his opinion. According to Jay Robert Nash, the verbally challenged Battaglia took the fifth amendment sixty times when being questioned before the McClellan committee because... "his diction was so poor that he would appear to be the moron he really was" (1930s-1970s).

*

"Dice, horses, women got everything we made — mostly dice."

Lawrence "Tiny" Mazzanars was not the only person to lament losing his fortune in this manner. Tiny, who was a member of the Chicago Bookie Gang in the 1940s, made hundreds of thousands of dollars through theft, robbery and murder, but in the end, wound up broke.

*

"I fix the price of beer in this town."

Alfred "Jake" Lingle, the infamous *Chicago Tribune* reporter and Capone Stooge. The corrupt reporter was cut down reportedly by Capone hired hit-man, Leo V. "Buster" Brothers (1930).

*

"The man with the revolver came close to the other fellow and aimed. Just as he fired the man jumped to one side. The bullet smashed the window of my store. Then the man fired again and the fellow he aimed at ducked his head forward. The third shot made a hole in my window."

This is Fritz Heiney's recollection of the assassination attempt on New York Mafia boss Joe "The Boss" Masseria by rival Peter Morello's gunman, Umberto Valenti. The incident occurred in Fritz's hat shop; Masseria, trapped in the shop after running for cover, dodged over ten bullets point blank while knocking over women's hats, scarves and other articles. When police arrived at "dancing" Joe's home to interview him about the shooting, Joe was found with his feet soaking in hot salted water, holding on to a clattering cup of chamomile while still wearing his bullet ventilated hat. Obviously the bullet-induced dance had caused the old don's corns to ache a tad (August 9, 1922).

*

> *"As soon as I finished drying my hands, I hurried out and walked back to see what it [the gun-fire] was about."*

As Lucky Luciano excused himself from his card game with Joe The Boss to go to the bathroom, Lucky's goons walked in a put six bullets into the back of Joe's head. When police arrived, Lucky had dry hands and an airtight alibi. This was Lucky's comment as quoted by the newspapers, but the prudish dailies refused to print his actual comment which would reveal Lucky's unlucky prostate problems. It was: "I was in the can taking a leak. I always take a long leak" (Scarpato's Restaurant, Cony Island, April 15, 1931).

*

> *"Don Vincenzo, tell your* compare *Maranzano that we have killed Masseria — not to serve him but for our own personal reasons. Tell him that if he should touch even the hair of even a personal enemy of ours we will wage war to the end."*

This was the stern message that Lucky Luciano had lackey Vincent Troia deliver to Salvatore Maranzano. The murder of Joe the Boss was the beginning of Luciano's elimination of the "Mustache Petes" (old world Mafiosi) and the restructuring and consolidation of power into what was to become "The (National Crime) Syndicate" and the Americanization of the Mafia. Luciano wanted nothing to interfere with his plans and he always backed his threats with action (April, 1931).

*

"This represents that you live by the gun and a knife... and you die by the gun and the knife."

During the Senate Investigations Subcommittee hearings, Joseph Valachi re-lived his initiation rites into "La Cosa Nostra" when he recited these verses from the ceremony given to him by mob boss Salvatore Maranzano (1962).

*

"Charlie, I've been waiting for this day for at least eight years. You're gonna be on top if I have to kill everybody for you. With you there, that's the only way we can have any peace and make the real money."

Albert Anastasia, the dreaded lord-high executioner of Murder Inc. (the muscle subsidiary of the Crime Syndicate), knew that Lucky Luciano was his ticket to the top. Albert helped wipe out a mob of Mafiosi, including Joe Masseria, Maranzano and many other Mustache Petes, ensuring Luciano's consolidation of power. On October 25, 1957, while Albert was reclining in a barber's chair with a pile of hot towels covering his face, he was shot dead, reportedly by fledglings Joe and Larry Gallo.

*

"Go to hell and take that greasy pimp boss of yours with you."

Manhattan whore master Pete Harris had brave words to offer when he was asked to pay his extortion fees by 'Lucky' Luciano's dapper thugs. As Luciano began to consolidate his control of the gambling and prostitution rackets in the Manhattan area during the early 1920s, a number of independent-minded operators refused to pay. When Pete Harris adamantly refused to pay cash, he wound up paying with his life. As a convincing example to other pimping mavericks, he was systematically perforated over a hundred times with an ice pick and then dumped into a stinking, sopping sewage ditch (not the same ditch Lucky was to occupy).

*

"Look, I'm pals with everybody. Nobody's after me. Everybody likes me."

Lucky Luciano had a strange sense of friendship. In October of 1929, Lucky was forced into a car and pounded for over half an hour by four thugs, slashed in the throat, ice picked several times in the back and then dumped in a sewage ditch, figured for dead. Lucky survived but his face required over forty painful stitches.

*

"Whores is whores, they can always be handled. They ain't got no guts."

Lucky Luciano, who earned over $10,000,000 a year from prostitution, had absolutely no respect for his hard working gals. Lucky had them beaten, cheated, and robbed out of their earnings while forcing them to live in seedy cockroach infested conditions. But, in 1935, Luciano lost his grip on their handles and three of his flatback molls, Nancy Presser, Cokey Flo Braun and Mildred Harris came forward and gave sterling court testimony which helped convict Lucky of compulsory prostitution, resulting in a thirty to fifty year sentence. Lucky was eventually released and deported to Italy in 1946 for "aiding" the U.S.A. in the war effort.

*

"Who do you think you are, Rudolph Valentino?"

Lucky Luciano and Joe Adonis competed not only for power, but also on personal appearance. In fact, Joey A. was so enamoured with his own looks that he changed his name from Giuseppe Doto to Joe Adonis (the youth the god Aphrodite loved for his beauty). One day while Adonis was preening and admiring himself in the mirror, Luciano spat out this envious crack to Adonis. Joe, who knew better than to upset the powerful Luciano but still needed to vent, meekly whispered, "For looks, that guy's a bum" (1930s).

*

"I have no plans to look him up and I hope he doesn't look me up."

Joe Adonis dodged the law by hiring expensive lawyers and using various fall guys to take the heat, but during his twenty-five year reign as one of New York's top crime bosses, not once did he figure on getting his American citizenship. Then on January 3rd, 1956, the non-American Adonis was deported to Italy for relatively insignificant gambling charges. While boarding the luxury liner SS Conte Biancamano (Count Whitehand-irony yes?) to Italy, he was asked by reporters if he would hook up with Lucky Luciano who had been deported in 1946. Adonis responded with customary indignation, perhaps too embarrassed to face the man he had ridiculed for the exact predicament he was now in himself.

*

"The millions Joey A. took out of the country didn't do him a damn bit of good in the end. He wade through blood to get it and he croaked with empty pockets in a dirty shack."

The gap toothed self proclaimed god of beauty, Adonis, who earned millions of dollars from the blood and lives of others, died in the humiliation he deserved. Sometime in 1972, the crime boss was unceremoniously yanked from his Milan villa by Italian police and taken to a remote squalid shack in the hills for questioning. (Italian authorities were involved in an extensive Mafia crack-down at the time.) Once in police custody the details of the remaining events remain sketchy, but Adonis, perhaps under the strain of questioning, guilt or self indignity, reportedly died of heart failure.

*

"Treat the sucker right, he is paying your salary. His stupidity is our income. You must never insult him, just cheat him with a smile... We'll make you rich, play the waiting game... keep your name out of the newspapers and build your own organization."

Arnold Rothstein and Meyer Lansky, respectively, were both brilliant business minded mobsters who were well ahead of their time. They developed and used a variety of business techniques which are now being used by the corporate world's top businessmen, only difference being that today's executives have experienced spin doctors convincing us that what they do is legal and morally correct (1920-30s).

*

"You want to know how I make my money? There are two million fools born for every intelligent man. That ought to answer you."

The contemptuously brilliant underworld businessman and gambling czar Arnold Rothstein knew that to make a buck, all he had to do was give the paying customers what he told them they wanted (1920s).

*

"Who cares about this stuff? This is America, not Jerusalem. I'm an American. Let Harry be a Jew."

When Arnold "The Brains" Rothstein was growing up, he did not get along well with his brother Harry. Harry, who later became a Rabbi, was the perfect Jewish son that Arnold could never be. Instead, Arnold wanted to be an American, he believed in the American tradition of free enterprise, opportunity and the whole rags-to-riches story upon which the foundation of the country stood. Before long, Arnold was living proof of the American dream — holding incredible power within the Mafia and making millions of dollars through illegal gambling, loan-sharking and rigged sporting events (1920s).

*

"I don't carry that kind of dough under my finger-nails."

Arnold Rothstein (a.k.a. Mr. Big) was a powerful mob business genius who made millions in gambling and fixing sporting events, the most famous being the 1919 World Series. But as the late 1920s approached, Mr. Big found that his good luck and fortune were vaporizing. In one particular incident while playing cards, Mr. Big lost big, over $300,000, much of it on poker and a number of adrenaline pumping $50,000 high card draws. When asked to pay up, he refused, adding to the above, "I don't pay off on fixed poker." About two months later, on November 4, 1928, after a continual string of nasty gambling losses, Rothstein was shot dead by unknown assailants.

*

"That's the last time a Jew will cheat a Sicilian in this town."

Business is business and personal cultural ties can go to hell, for Meyer Lansky anyway. Lansky, a Jew himself, knew where the muscle and money was so it would have been insane for him to back fellow Jew Louis "Russian Louie" Strauss after Strauss had skimmed money from mob casinos. Strauss was strangled and buried for his troubles, but they couldn't bury his name. In Las Vegas there is a saying when money is owed that goes… "I'll pay when Russian Louie hits town" (1930s).

*

"He would have been chairman of the board of General Motors if he'd gone into legitimate business."

This comment was made by an FBI agent on the undisputed underworld crime mastermind Meyer Lansky.

*

"Take care of this guy."

When Meyer Lansky gave this order to his noxious colleagues, he wasn't implying that "this guy" be booked into some swank Las Vegas hotel with a bevy of randy escorts, he meant for the guy to be immediately purged from society. In November of 1939, Lansky issued Bugsy Siegal this directive on Harry "Big Greenie" Greenberg. Big Greenie had broken two of the mob's most sacred rules; he stole mob money and turned informant. So later that month, Siegel, along with Frankie Carbo, Allie Tannenbaum and Whitey Krakower, took care of Greenberg.

*

"We loaded a carload of goods, got our cash, and shipped it. We shipped a lot of goods. I never went to the other side of the border to count the empty Seagram's bottles."

During prohibition, Samuel Bronfman made an incredible fortune selling vast amounts of legal Canadian booze to American bootleggers including Meyer Lansky, Moe Dalitz and Lucky Luciano. Throughout the operation, there was a clandestine free trade agreement between the parties where the alcohol was exchanged for huge sacks of cash. When prohibition ended in 1933, the U.S. government was not privy to their agreement and demanded over $60 million in back taxes from the Canadians on the alcohol shipped. After lengthy negotiations, the Americans settled for $3 million of which Bronfman graciously allowed the Canadian government to pay half.

*

"Well, you son of a bitch, you had it coming to you. What do you think of it? You gave it to a lot

*of other guys yourself? How do you like it your-
self?"*

Small time punk Louis Kushner under orders from
"Legs" Diamond and Louis Buchalter shot Manhattan
racketeering overlord Nathan "Kid Dropper" Kaplan
straight-away in the head. Kaplan, at the time, was stuck
in a traffic-blocked cab being escorted out of New York
by police Captain Willemse. As Kaplan rolled on the cab
floor whimpering like the pathetic coward that he was,
police Captain Willemse whispered these last words of
comfort into his ear (August 28, 1923).

*

"The fix is in, you'll see."

Right up to the time he got up to start walking to
the electric chair at Sing Sing, Mob boss Louis "Lepke"
Buchalter tried to convince co-accused Louis Capone
(no relation to Al) and Mendy Weiss that they were
certain to be pardoned of the murder of Joseph Rosen.
Buchalter figured that he and his buddies would be saved
through the influence of his powerful mob associates,
instead, Lepke was betrayed by those he served loyally.
On March 4, 1944, after New York governor Thomas E.
Dewey refused any further requests for a stay, Lepke and
his pals were seared by over 2,200 volts of electricity.

*

"I never heard of Albert Anastasia. How could you couple my name in the same breath."

During his murder trial, the zealous murderer Frank Abbandando became personally offended when his own name was linked with that of the Murder Inc. boss Albert Anastasia. During court testimony, turncoat Kid Twist Reles described in gory detail how Frank, along with some of his brutes mercilessly murdered loan shark George "Whitey" Rudnick. According to Reles, Rudnick was stabbed sixty-three times with an ice pick, strangled and then had his head pounded to a pulp with a meat cleaver. One could only speculate why Frank felt offended by being associated with Anastasia, perhaps Albert used a dull meat cleaver (1940).

*

"The skull and crossbones of the underworld must come down."

During his murder trial, the cold and clinical Frank 'The Dasher' Abbandando openly threatened presiding Judge Franklin W. Taylor while giving testimony. Even though Judge Taylor was out to stop organized crime, he feared for his life and ordered an armed guard stationed between himself and The Dasher (1942).

*

"Well, that one doesn't count really, I married the girl later."

During his murder trial, Abbandando, a proud perpetual rapist by nature, denied raping anyone. When the prosecutor reminded The Dasher that earlier he had practically admitted to raping a particular woman, Frank tried to argue that his actions were in fact just pre-nuptial courting rituals (1942).

*

"I'm gonna be eatin' spaghetti at home on Sunday."

Just before the murder trial, the overconfident Abbandando was sure that his top mobster associates, which included Adonis, Buchalter and Anastasia, were going to rig the jury in his favour, instead, Frank was in for the shock of his life. The jury found Frank guilty of first degree murder and sentenced him to die strapped to the electric chair at Sing Sing. While awaiting his execution, the ever sanguine Abbandando told reporters, "I'm gonna miss the first night ball game of the season." Frank fried on February 19, 1942.

*

"Don't touch me. Call the cops, but don't touch me. I'll kill you if you do."

Vito Genovese, even when a young boy, showed the characteristics of the future Mafia Don he was to become. After being caught stealing a banana from a street vendor, Vito held his ground and refused to be manhandled by the lowly peddler, he didn't want to get his threads wrinkled (1910s).

*

"I'm only going out for a few minutes, besides, I'm wearing thermal underwear."

As the Genovese crime family lieutenant Tony Bender was leaving his home in the morning, his wife was concerned that the chill in the air would make him ill, but, in reality, Bender would need more than warm underwear to keep his skin from getting cold and clammy. On that morning of April 8, 1962, Bender disappeared and was never heard from again. Speculation in the industry has it that under Genovese's orders Tony was tossed into a batch of concrete, perhaps to increase its compressive strength and then poured into the foundation of some famous Manhattan Skyscraper. Other accounts have Bender being mixed in as an asphalt substitute and used to pave the West Side Highway. More digging to confirm his location and physical state is necessary.

*

"Other kids are brought up nice and sent to Harvard or Yale. Me? I was brought up like a mushroom."

Frank Costello grew up in the squalid, overcrowded, lice ridden conditions of the East Harlem ghetto. The sheer poverty and hopelessness of the area proved to be a fertile training ground for many future high profile gangsters. Frank, who in a baneful way benefited from his early surroundings, had so much resentment for his poor childhood that he swore he would become a respectable "suit and tie" crook (1950s).

*

"I never wanted a piece of paper so bad in my life. The old bat nagged me to death all my life. It was always: 'Frank, why don't you go straight?' She always swore she never did anything wrong in her life. I wanted that piece of paper to show her how she had beat this poor old guy out of two sacks of flour."

Frank "The Prime Minister" Costello, National Crime Syndicate cofounder and underworld overlord, was continually being tormented by his nagging mother to get an honest job. But in 1927, when Frank went back to his home town of Lauropoli in Italy for a visit, he got satisfaction. While handing out the green, as was custom of "done good" expatriates, a meek old timer handed him an IOU for two sacks of flour that his mother had signed thirty-five years earlier. Frank paid the man generously and now had the ammunition to get his mother off his back.

*

"It's cost us a hundred grand, but Kid Twist Reles is about to join his maker."

The mysterious death of informant Kid Twist Reles has always been shrouded in fog. While under heavy police protection at the Half Moon Hotel in Coney Island, Reles fell? out of a sixth floor window onto the hard pavement below. In an interview a number of years later, Doc Stacher reminisced when Frank Costello announced the impending doom of the heavily guarded stoolie Reles. Costello knew so many top level police officials that it became only a matter of negotiating the price of $100,000 to get the job done (1941).

*

"I'm called the Burglar's Lobby in Washington because I defend people like Frank Costello. The Sixth Amendment of the Constitution guarantees the right of legal counsel to everyone, it does not say to everyone except people like Frank Costello."

Defense Lawyer Edward Bennett Williams defended many mobsters or mob related causes with great success, including the acquittal of Jimmy Hoffa and the overturning of Frank Costello's deportation order. Williams liked to hide behind his Sixth Amendment argument to defend his own diluted morals which he used as justification in defending mobsters for huge sums of money.

*

"I got to be careful of my associates. They'll accuse me of consortin' with questionable characters."

Frank Costello often indirectly provided FBI director and horse junkie J. Edgar Hoover with winning tips on fixed horse races. Frank had his own business interests in mind when helping Hoover but when he encountered the dim director in Toots Shor's nightclub one evening, he had to make sure that Hoover wasn't getting the wrong impression by thinking they were pals (1950s).

*

"Because I love this country."

The All-American killer-jingoist Frank Costello brought patriotic tears to the eyes of the Kefauver Committee members when they asked him why he had become an American citizen. Of course Frank loved America, what other country could afford to give a sharpie such an opportunity into the big time (1950-51).

*

"I'm sorry, counselor, I'd rather blow the goddamn case."

During one of his court appearances, the dapper Frank was advised by his paid mouthpiece (a.k.a. lawyer) to wear a standard off the rack suit in court, instead of his custom cuts. This, to improve his image with the jury. Costello refused, preferring to be in a tight cell than an ill fitting suit (1950s).

*

"This is for you, Frank."

Just as a bullet put a crease in his skull, the dapper New York racketeer Frank Costello was greeted by Vincent "The Chin" Gigante. Either by plan or mistake, The Chin missed but the objective was reached, Frank got the message and started divesting his gambling and racketeering interests and quickly went into retirement. Retirement suited Frank and he enjoyed the role as a celebrity ex-gangster, hanging out and bragging about his past exploits in Toots Shor's Nightclub (May 2, 1957).

*

"You'll be drowned in your own soup."

When a group of Brownsville cafeteria workers decided to strike in 1933, management figured that the only way to settle the dispute quickly was to bring in labour racketeer "negotiator" and mob killer extraordinaire Kid Twist Reles. The incessant killer met with the workers and outlined the consequences of continuing their action. The strike ended abruptly and Reles was paid an $8,500 "consulting fee."

*

"Pep ain't gonna like his garage all messed up like this."

After having blown away the heads of Joe Amberg and his chauffeur Mannie Kellser, Murder Inc.'s hygienic killer Harry Maione was concerned about the cranial mess on the floor of Pep's (Pittsburgh Phil's) garage. Harry didn't wanna be the one to have to mop up the mess (September 30, 1935).

*

"How come you keep writing all those bad things about my brother Albert? He ain't killed nobody in your family yet!"

Tough talking Tony Anastasio intimidated others by using the influence he gained from his murderous brother and Murder Inc. director Albert Anastasia (changed his name to protect his family back in Italy). Tony fed his ego and got his thrills by threatening small time reporters and other indefensible individuals at his whim. When his brother Albert was slaughtered in 1957, Tony cried for days, not so much because he lost his brother, but because he lost his brother's influence, leaving him nothing to do but look over his shoulder. Mercifully, Tony died of natural causes in 1963.

*

"I never heard him say a bad word in front of me or the children. He never spoke roughly... He used to go to church with me every Sunday. He gave generously to the church... Now he's not even buried in consecrated ground."

When murderer and overlord of Murder Incorporated Albert Anastasia was blasted to death, his wife Elsa could not believe what was being said and written about her husband. Elsa fervently claimed that Albert was the ideal husband; he never drank, was always good to the children, enjoyed socializing and was always home by 9 pm. But soon after his death, Elsa cashed in the assets, changed the family's name and moved to Canada (October, 1957).

*

"I don't trust that Legs. He's nuts. He gets excited and starts pulling a trigger like another guy wipes his nose."

Dutch Schulz on Legs Diamond (1929).

*

"I don't trust the Dutchman. He's a crocodile. He's sneaky. I don't trust him."

Legs Diamond on Dutch Schultz (1929).

*

"Can't anybody shoot that guy so he won't bounce back up."

An aggravated Dutch Schultz just couldn't figure out what it would take to kill his bootlegging arch enemy Jack Legs Diamond, known by many as the clay pigeon of the underworld. Whenever an attempt was made on the Diamond's life, he was able to rebound back stronger than ever. Here is a sample of what the Diamond was able to absorb.

In the early 1920s, Diamond took bullets to his arms and legs while acting as a body guard for Little Augie Orgen.

In 1924, he was shot in the head and foot with buckshot during an ambush. He casually drove himself to the hospital for treatment.

In October of 1927, Diamond was shot full of so many holes during Little Augie's assassination that he was given his last rites; he dumbfounded the priest, doctors and his assassins by surviving.

In October of 1930, Diamond was filled with a steam of lead while intimately tucked under with his mistress Kiki Roberts. Again he was given last rites and again he stunned those involved by surviving.

In April of 1931, while coming out of an ale house, he was plugged again, this time in the back, lung, liver and arm. Confounding his would be killers, the doctors and anyone else who heard of the incident, he again survived.

After a while, he become so cocky of his own invincibility that when he was told that a group of brutal rat-like thugs were out to nail him, he replied, "What the hell do I care? The bullet hasn't been made that can kill me." On December 17, 1931, the Diamond was put into his final setting; while in a drunken sleep, two gunmen entered his room, grabbed him by the ears, pressed their guns to his head and shot him three times. As of late last week, reports indicate that Legs Diamond is still dead.

*

"Look, I want the Mick killed. He's driving me out of my mind. I'll give a house in Winchester to any of you guys who knocks him off."

Dutch Schultz had the nerve to offer the detectives of the Morrisania Precinct Station in New York a house if they would kill Vincent "Mad Dog" Coll, the rebel gangster who was trying to take over Dutch's bootleg territory. This act alone was clear testimony to the power and influence he, along with many other crime barons held over the law during that period. After being mildly reprimanded by the detectives, Dutchie replied almost apologetically, "I just came in to tell you that I'll pay good to any cop who kills the Mick!" (1930s.)

*

'You miserable bum! I'll shove that dough down your throat!"

New York police detective Steve DiRosa had to be pulled off Dutch Schultz by his partner as he tried to shove a wad of cash down the Dutchman's throat. Schultz had mistook DiRosa in a dark alley as his arch nemesis Mad Dog Coll and shot at the detective a number of times. When Dutch discovered what he had done, he tried to bribe his way out of it with over $18,000 in cash he was carrying in his suit pocket. The magnanimous DiRosa didn't take offense, he just wanted to safely return the cash (June 1931).

*

"You can insult Arthur's girl, spit in his face, push him around and he'll laugh. But don't steal a dollar from his accounts. If you do, you're dead."

Dixie Davis, Dutch Shultz's fawning lawyer, clearly outlined that Schultz, a true Dutchman at heart, may have been willing to go Dutch with his girl, but never with his money.

*

"I have been charged with all kinds of crimes but, baby, killing was the limit. I'd like nothing better than to lay my hands on the man who did this. I'd tear his throat out. There is nothing more despicable than a man who would harm an innocent child."

Mad Dog Coll was acquitted of murdering five year old Michael Vengali, through the cunning and underhanded methods of his grease-ball lawyer Samuel Leibowitz. Coll had killed Michael and injured three other children while trying to machine gun down Joey and Vincent Rao on July 23, 1931.

*

"That yellow rat, Schultz! I'm gonna burn that Dutch man to hell!"

When the vicious and mentally unhinged bootlegger and child killer Mad Dog Coll discovered that his brother Peter was killed by Dutch Schultz, he swore a vengeance that was never to materialize. Coll was at one time a Dutch Schultz enforcer who splintered off when Schultz refused to cut him in on the action. Angry at the brush-off, Coll waged a gangland war with Schultz that resulted in a harvest of gunmen's bodies from both gangs clogging the gutters of New York. Then, on February 7, 1932, as the Mad Dog was on the phone in a drug store phone booth trying to extort money from Owney "The Killer" Madden, one of Schultz's gunmen walked into the drugstore quietly and told the customers, "All keep quiet. Keep cool now" and proceeded to unleash a volley of machine gun fire that left Coll and the phone booth in a shredded mass of tissue, metal and glass.

*

"The first thing you'll see in my area is this gun, Dutch, and it'll be the last thing you'll see."

Dutch Schutlz was the enterprising type who was always looking to expand his operations. One day when he approached Louis "Pretty" Amberg with an offer to become a partner in Amberg's territory, Pretty responded with indignation. On October 23, 1935, under the orders of Buchalter and Anastasia, Murder Inc. sent its top "mediators" to remove Amberg from the territory. When they got hold of Pretty they carved him up like a Halloween pumpkin and then blew the back of his head off, burning his remains to ashes in a car doused with gasoline. The druid-like ceremonial cremation was ignited by a buxom blonde from a randy group who had drawn for the short straw. The pyre-blonde was later named Miss Murder Inc. by the participating mobsters for her efforts.

*

"Personally, I think only queers wear silk shirts... I never bought one in my life. A guy's a sucker to spend $15 or $20 on a shirt. Hell, a guy can get a good one for two bucks."

After Dutch Schultz was charged with tax evasion in 1932, his lawyer Dixie Davis had the case moved to a small town, the idea being to con the locals into thinking that the Dutchman was really a swell guy. Schultz played the role of the small town hick perfectly by going to county fairs, cleaning out barns and making statements like this one. By trial time, the jury comprised of local residents was completely whitewashed and subsequently cleared the Dutchman of all charges. Lucky Luciano was later to comment on the deceased Schultz's dress code: "The guy had a couple of million bucks and he dressed like a pig."

*

"Please crack down on the Chinaman's friends and Hitler's commander. I am sure and I am going up and I am going to give you honey, if I can. Mother is the best and don't let Satan draw you too fast... Shut up! You got a big mouth! Please help me up, Henry. Max, come over here! French Canadian bean soup. I want to pay. Let them leave me alone..."

On October 23, 1935, while tending to his regular ablutions, Dutch Schultz was ambushed in the bathroom of the Palace Chop House in Newark, New Jersey by hired gunman Charles "The Bug" Workman. While dying in his hospital bed for over two days, police stenographer F. J Long took an endless dictation of useless babble, hoping for shreds of incriminating dialogue to appear that could be used against his associates. None was recovered.

*

"I cannot speak for the jury, but I believe if there were even a shred of corroborating evidence you would have been condemned to the electric chair. By devious means, among which were the terrorizing of witnesses, kidnapping them, yes, even murdering those who would give evidence against you, you have thwarted justice time and again."

When Vito Genovese was acquitted of the murder of Ferdinand Boccia, due to the lack of living witnesses, Judge Samuel Leibowitz made it clear to the court that he was aware of how the Mafia operated. Early in his career, Judge Leibowitz had been an accomplished criminal lawyer; he learned of the mob's inner cabal by defending a number of brutally vicious criminals such as Mad Dog Coll. It seems ironic that Leibowitz should have been upset at Genovese being acquitted when, as a lawyer, he used his own questionable court room tactics to achieve the same results (June 11, 1946).

*

"He was a good father who raised his children to be honest, well-behaved and religious."

The very tactful and self preserving police captain James Egido said this about one of the most ruthlessly dangerous and murderous men to reach the pinnacle of Mafia power. Vito Genovese, who would think nothing of double crossing friends or murdering business partners, would always be at home in the evening to spend time with his family and to plan out his criminal activities. This comment was made while Vito was serving a fifteen year sentence on a narcotics conviction (1960s).

*

"I'm gonna make you an offer you can't refuse."

Funky New Jersey crime boss Willie Moretti was perhaps the first real manager Frank Sinatra had. In the early 1930s, Willie discovered Frank crooning in a seedy New Jersey dive and knew that Frank could do better, so by using his influence he soon had Sinatra entertaining tony audiences in swank clubs all around town. In 1939, Sinatra had an opportunity for a part in a Hollywood movie but was refused a contract release by his bandleader Tommy Dorsey. Willie paid Dorsey a visit and settled the matter by jamming a loaded gun into Dorsey's mouth and offering him $1.00 for Sinatra's contract. It was either his signature or skull fragments on the contract. Dorsey inked the deal.

*

"I'm not a member of the Mafia because I do not have a membership card."

Willie Moretti was a gangster and enforcer with a twisted sense of humour. When he was asked by the Kefauver Committee if he was in the Mafia, Willie checked his wallet and gave this witty reply (1950-51).

*

"Don't forget my house in Deal if you are down on the shore. You are invited."

When the affable racketeer Willie Moretti had completed his testimony to the Kefauver committee hearings, he promptly invited all the Senators to his waterfront retreat. Problem was, Willie wasn't going to be around much longer to entertain his guests (1951).

*

"They call anybody a mobster who makes six percent more on money."

During Moretti's testimony Senator Charles Tobey stated that Willie's responses were quite refreshing. But like any financial extortionist worth his wingtips, Willie knew that the goal of any investor was to maximize the return on investment and, since his financial services company catered to a riskier clientele which other institutions wouldn't touch, he felt justified in demanding a higher interest rate or "risk" premium.

*

"If tomorrow I go wrong, I would want to be hit so as not to bring harm to this thing of ours."

This was part of Vito Genovese's argument in front of the Commissione, or Mafia Board of Directors to have syphilitic New Jersey racket boss Willie Moretti eliminated. Willie, a humorous fellow at times, had "gone soft in the head, like the inside of a melon" according to Genovese, and had to be silenced before he said too much. On Oct. 4, 1951, Willie was shot to death in Joe's restaurant in Cliffside Park, N.J. before he could finish eating his lunch.

*

"Buster looked like a college kid, a little over six feet, light complexion, weighed about 200 pounds. He would also carry a violin case."

According to Joseph Valachi, Buster from Chicago was one of the most prolific of underworld assassins at the time, the Wayne Gretzky of killers. Imported from Chicago, Buster carried his Tommy Gun, attachments and other gadgets of death in a customized hard leather violin case. In September of 1931, Buster was "dispatched" under orders from Luciano and Genovese for being a potential threat to their own health, should he be hired by their enemies.

*

"Twenty seven contracts ended in complete misses, slight wounds, and bodies being left around in the street."

Joseph Valachi's testimony to a Senate Investigations Subcommittee gave the public an idea of the extent to which the mob's hit-men screwed up. Scared, blathering would-be corpses, flopping bloody bodies and messy cringed cadavers scattered all about would not be tolerated by the bosses; they ran a clean business and had their reputation to maintain. According to Valachi, some of the more klutzy mob hit-men were eventually reas-signed to lighter, more "earthy" duties.

*

"You imagine my embarrassment when I killed the wrong guy."

When Joe Valachi killed innocent hapless bystand-ers, it was his reputation he was worried about and not the dead victim. Just think about it, Joe hanging with his goomba pals and having to bear their endless taunts on his murderous screw ups. I bet Joe felt like crawling under one of his slimy rocks (Senate hearings, 1962).

*

"Sam had an iron pipe hammered up his ass."

According to Valachi, Maranzano Lieutenant Sam Monaco was "paid a visit" by a very unethical, and perhaps, unlicensed plumber. When Sam was found floating in Newark Bay, he had his throat slit, his head smashed and new galvanized accessories installed (1931).

*

"He tied up the artichokes in the city. The way I understand it, he would buy all the artichokes that came into New York... Being artichokes, they hold; they can keep. Then Ciro would make his own

price, and as you know, Italians got to have arti-chokes to eat."

There must be an infinite plus one number of ways to make crooked money. Diamonds? Yes! But who would have ever thought that there could be a racket in cornering the artichoke market. According to Joseph Valachi, Ciro Terranova, the squeamish and overrated mobster of New York controlled the artichoke markets using muscle supplied by the Morello Family. Who knows, anchovies may be next (1920s?).

*

"Someday the Mob is going to put a man in the White House and he's not going to know it until they present him with the Bill."

Joseph Valachi could not overstate the influence that organized crime had within the American political system. Valachi was just confirming what had been known for many years: the proliferation of ballot box rigging and voter intimidation, police and judicial pay-offs, questionable political contributions, shady criminal pardons, influence peddling, misuse of political powers for personal gain, judicial corruption, yada yada yada, the list goes on and on (3,500 BC to present).

*

"There's no chance you'll get killed. We only kill each other."

Bugsy Siegel had to reassure his Las Vegas contrac-tor Del Webb that there was nothing to worry about. Del was feeling pressure to complete Bugsy's over-budget and behind schedule Flamingo Hotel. The Mob funded Bugsy and was putting the heat on to see reult. Those problems, along with an unsuccessful opening, put the east coast Mob "financiers" on the edge, demanding their money back with interest. Bugsy scoffed and told Lucky Luciano to "go to hell." On June 20, 1947, while in the home of Virginia Hill, the man who had envisioned and created La Vegas was shot three times in the face; his left eye blown right out of its socket.

*

"Look in the deep freeze unit and get the package I left there. The one that came in today. Send it over right away."

The term "cold hard cash" may have been coined by the Genghis Khan of mob murderers, "Trigger" Mike Coppola. One night Coppola woke up in a cold sweat when he realized that he had left $219,000 of mob money in the meat freezer of a midtown New York social club. Apparently, Mike was involved in one of his intense card games and had iced the money for safekeeping and forgotten it. Mike scrambled to the phone at two in the morning and ordered a petrified clerk to deliver the money immediately. Mike knew that if that money was lost or stolen, he would have been the next one in a freezer (December 23, 1958).

*

"Go on and have your fun, I won't bump off any-body here tonight."

When the notorious New York crime boss and boot-legging murderer Owney "The Killer" Madden walked into a New York dance club, the orchestra on stage immediately froze solid with fear and stopped playing. Noticing the silence and the stares of many of the guests, the slim Madden waved his hand back in a contemptu-ous manner and told the band to resume playing as he headed towards a group of anxious, squirming gals (November 6, 1912).

*

"Come on, youse guys. Youse wouldn't shoot no-body! Who did you ever bump off?"

The terrible Owney was normally an alert, sharp eyed killer who constantly surveyed his surroundings for danger. But that evening, while distracted by the caresses of those beautiful ladies, the dashing Owney was quickly surrounded by eleven armed, brutal gunmen. As Owney stood up to face the thugs, their guns erupted and Owney took in eight slugs (1912).

*

"Nothing doing. The boys'll get 'em. It's nobody's business but mine who put these slugs into me!"

Even after he stopped those eight slugs with various parts of his body, Owney didn't do his assailants any favours by not revealing their names to the police. Instead, Owney saved the cops their time and the taxpayers their money by having his own goons hunt down and liquidate the punks who tried to kill him.

*

"Maybe I am getting lockjaw from getting bit."

Pittsburgh Phil, the repentless murderer was said to have a cemetery of head stones to his credit. On one occasion while ice picking his victim Puggy Feinstein to death, Puggy fought back valiantly and got in a few good chomps of Strauss' finger. Phil, perhaps a bit of a closet hypochondriac, was concerned that Puggy's bite would give him a bug that could make him ill.

*

"This man is a paid assassin. When you meet such men, draw quickly and shoot accurately."

New York City police Commissioner Lewis J. Valentine gave his men clear and precise instructions on how to handle the treacherous Pittsburgh Phil who had purportedly killed more than 500 men (1930s).

*

"Whaddya runnin' for? You run and somebody runs after you, Happy. We're just a couple of guys out for a stroll, walking nice and slow. We don't know that guy back there. He didn't know us...We're just a coupla visitors to the fair city of

Detroit, Hap. Come to see the new cars and the big factories. Yea, that's us. Tourists...That guy back there shot full of holes? Hell, we don't know a thing about it... we're just strangers in town lookin' for a good time."

Pittsburgh Phil, was the mob murderer with ice water blood, nerves of granite and the conscience of a weevil. After killing his assignment Harry Millman and injuring five other innocent diners by spraying gunfire in a crowded restaurant, he coolly walked out of the chaotic restaurant while at the same time ensuring that his understudy Harry "Happy" Maione stayed well composed (1937).

*

"Think of that. With this bum you gotta be a doctor or he floats."

Strauss was always looking for ways to become a more a more effective killer, an example of his ingenuity was with victim Walter Sage. Sage was killed then tied to a pinball machine and dumped into a lake for permanent disposal. But, after a while, the ropes loosened and gastric gasses that built up in the corpse caused it to rise to the surface. Strauss, becoming aware of this type of problem, made it a point to perforated the victim's stomach with an ice pick to ensure that the gasses that built up would escape (1937).

*

"Poochy, you shouldn't have interfered."

These were the final words spoken to Edward "Poochy" Walsh by the enthusiastically violent murderer Elmer "Trigger" Burke. During a bar fight between Burke and a Joseph Lancia, Poochy interfered and stopped Burke from killing Lancia. Poochy was rewarded with three bullets point blank, all compliments of Burke (1950s).

*

"Save my scrapbook, for history's sake."

Trigger Burke was just one of those guys who had a hankering for fully loaded machine guns. During his notorious career, he had compiled and maintained a personal scrapbook which contained over 140 newspaper articles, columns and photos detailing his barbarous accomplishments. Burke was finally convicted of murder and sentenced to die by electric chair on January 9, 1958, but just before being electrocuted, the stone faced, yet proud Burke made this final request to the guy at the lever.

*

"You used to be my boss, so I won't kill you now. I'm gonna give you enough scratch to take a powder. But if me or any of my boys ever see you in New York again, you're gonna be pushing up lilacs

in a cemetery and you'll go into a box with pennies on your eyelids!"

Waxey Gordon was not the most poetic gangster, but he made the consequences quite clear to Joseph "Joe the Greaser" Rosenberg. In the early 1910s, Joe had been a major New York labour racketeer and Tammany Hall man with over 100 mindless thugs who pounded disruptive "pinko" advocates and striking workers into submission. But, in 1914, Rosenberg was charged with murder and canned. On his release he tried to regain his territory only to have Waxey pull the plug (1924).

*

"Shoot me. Don't take me in for junk. Let me run, and then shoot me!"

By the time the 1950s rolled around, ex-millionaire bootlegging czar Waxey Gordon had fallen so low that he had to push drugs to make a living. After being arrested with just over $6,000 worth of heroine (the kind of money he used to spend on a pair of socks in the 1930s), Waxey begged to be dropped right there rather than be humiliated by such petty charges. Regardless, Waxey was convicted and sentenced to Alcatraz for twenty-five years. Totally broken, the enigmatic Waxey died on June 24, 1952, shortly after entering prison.

*

"I would have dragged the body around the corner to my place."

It's a known fact that competition for restaurant clientele in New York City is, quite literally, murder. So when mob boss Paul Castellano and his bodyguard Thomas Bilotti were shot to death practically on the doorsteps of New York's Sparks Steak House in 1985, a local competitor commented on what he should have done to cash in on the unexpected windfall. Later, as the packed restaurant started to empty, a satiated and belching client was asked why such a rush into Spark's, he commented, "I always eat at these places. Would Mafia Dons eat at a crummy Italian restaurant?"

*

"If you didn't eat it, you'd get your fingers broken."

The advertising campaign of Cous' Little Italy Restaurant in Philadelphia made you a menu offer you couldn't refuse. The burger was in honour of Philadelphia mob boss Philip "Chicken Man" Testa who used a chicken shop as a front for his more lucrative activities. In March of 1981, the Testa Burger was pulled from the menu when the Chicken Man was blown to giblets right on his own porch.

*

"Order something else."

On a good day, the harrowing Pretty Amberg was not a pleasant man to hang around with. Pretty, God's clear definition of ugly, was a human munitions dump who normally walked around armed with guns, clubs, brass knuckles, ice picks and a variety of other implements of pain and death. Often, when the stumpy goon was feeling particularly nasty, he would parade into restaurants and clear food laden tables, instructing the diners to make another selection from the menu (1930s).

*

"You know, we got a lot of laundry bags at the shop. You don't sign up with us you're gonna be in one of them bags."

Pretty usually extorted on the most vulnerable, and often used this convincing sales pitch to promote his Brooklyn linen service on otherwise reluctant restaurant owners. But one good thing you could say of Pretty, he could never be accused of false advertising. His claims were often backed up by newspaper accounts of the occasional corpse found floating in one of his blood soaked laundry bags (1930s).

*

"This is strictly a cement overcoat situation."

The transportation rackets netted the "syndicate" incredible sums of money. When a New York banana importer was asked by some nosey, trouble-making scribe about being forced to use an overpriced mob trucking firm to transport his bananas, the importer replied with the standard sound-bite.

*

"Hats off, you Jews, when you're passing the house of God, or I'll shoot them off."

While hijacking a beer truck from some Jewish crooks, the deistic murderous bootlegger Terry Druggan took the time to instruct his temporary hostages the religious decorum to be respected as they passed a Christian church (1920s).

*

"This cash is for the usual considerations and conveniences."

As soon as Chicago trigger happy swill sellers Terry Druggan and partner Frankie Lake entered prison for brewery violations, they handed the crooked sheriff Peter Hoffam $20,000 in cash to make their stay in the slammer a little more tolerable (1924).

*

"Mr. Druggan and Mr. Lake are out right now... an appointment downtown. They'll return after dinner."

When a reporter called the prison to interview the two mobsters, the response by sheriff Hoffman's secretary caught the reporter totally off guard. After the story went public on how the gangsters received red carpet treatment as a result of their payoff, the sheriff was sentenced to thirty days and fined $2,500. When the upset sheriff was placed in his own jail-cell he blurted out, "I don't know what the fuss is all about — I was only accommodatin' the boys."

*

"I'm a hoodlum. I don't want to be a legitimate guy. All these other racket guys who get a few bucks want to become legitimate."

New Jersey extortionist and loan shark Gyp De-Carlo had no illusions, he knew what he wanted to be from the time he was five years old. Focused and determined, DeCarlo methodically made his way to the top by climbing up the pile of dead bodies of his competitors and enemies, with helping boosts from various politicos, including President Richard M. Nixon, Newark Mayor Hugh Adonizio and Hudson political boss John Kenny.

*

"Let me hit you clean... Now listen, you gotta go. Why not let me hit you right in the heart and you

won't feel a thing?" Reply: *"I'm innocent... but if you gotta do it..."*

Gyp DeCarlo sometimes had a soft spot when it came to killing. Before this murder, he consulted with his victim to ensure that the poor sod was fully informed and wouldn't get all stressed out about the "procedure." After the consultation, the victim was shot in the heart and died instantly, the bullet gong clear through the body (1960s).

*

"In this way I found peace of mind because nobody would be able to do away with my person."

Nicola Gentile, who hoped to mimic the sophisticated English he'd been exposed to in high society dives, expressed great relief after he fell under the protective umbrella of a Brooklyn mob family (1930s).

*

"I want you to kill every cop in the city. Now, right now... You'll kill a cop, I give you two hundred and fifty dollars, right away. Just make sure you kill him, not just hurt him. He never gets up again. Dead."

These were the orders issued by the audacious Akron Ohio mob boss Rosario Borgio who decided to wipe out the local police force because he was unable to buy them off. Shortly after, one by one, a number of policemen were murdered without warning, usually by being shot in the back. But an anonymous tip eventually led the baffled detectives to the necrotic Borgio who ended up frying on the electric chair (1910s).

*

"Well, you'd better get a lot more because we're going to kill him and you'll need it."

Sometime near the end of 1926, bootlegger Charles Birger discovered that West City Ill. Mayor Joe Adams had switched his loyalty to the rival Shelton Gang. Seeking revenge with the mayor, but giving full consideration to the Adams' family financial well-being, Birger called up the Mayor's wife and informed her that she should beef up her husband's insurance policy and make sure it included a rider for the grim "lead flu" that was going around. On December 12, 1926, Charles had his gunmen Harry and Elmo Thomasson kill Adams in his own home, right in front of the Mayor's hysterical wife.

*

"Never did see so many ugly people in my life…"

As Charles Birger peered through his barred window onto the prison yard where he was soon to hang for the murder of Adams, he scanned the hordes of eager rubber-neckers who had come to watch him swing in the early morning chill. Maintaining his indignation to the end, the appalling murderer had to get a final cheap shot at the crowd. Then, noticing the smiles on the guards faces, he retorted: "They're no better looking than you fellows" (April 19, 1928).

*

"If he's a gangster, I wish all of them were."

Mob boss, racketeer and multiple murderer Tommy "Three Fingers" Luchese was a charmer, who mingled with the social elite, which included top judges, members of congress, and other well heeled wannabes. By the time Luchsee died in 1967, he had so completely whitewashed these folks that this comment reflected their general belief and lunacy.

*

"The rats! They tried to wipe out my family!"

In the final seconds of his life, while full of machine gun lead, the delirious Brooklyn bootlegger Vannie Higgins sprang up in his hospital bed, declared his conspiracy theory and dropped dead. Earlier that day, Vannie and his family were attacked by a carload of machine gun laden thugs. As his wife and daughter ran for cover, Vannie, with only a pistol in his hand and even less in his head, chased the car on foot only to be hit by a blizzard of hot bullets (June 18, 1932).

*

"Doc, what I can't understand is why anybody would do this to me? Why to me, to Johnny Lazia, who has been the friend of everybody?"

Kansas City crime Czar Johnny Lazia, must have been a few bullets shy of a loaded gun. He just couldn't figure that his involvement in murder, extortion, election strong-arming, racketeering and various other criminal activities may have been the reason why a couple of Tommy gun drums were emptied into his body (July 10, 1934).

*

"Hell, the worst I can get is life."

Iowa swill pusher and racketeer Dave "Davie the Jew" Berman was arrested in May of 1927, for the kidnapping of New York bootlegger Abraham Scharlin. After weeks of heavy questioning by police, these were Davie's only words. Davie was found guilty and served just over seven years in Sing Sing.

*

"I am just a low, uncouth person. I'm a low-type sort of man."

Hollywood extortionist Willie Morris Bioff agreed to testify against a number of mob bosses after being sentenced to ten years for racketeering in 1941. Willie's testimony convicted a number of Chicago bosses including Frank Nitti, Paul Ricca and Phil Andrea. After his release, Bioff, who had trouble staying away from the action, worked at the Riviera in Las Vegas under the name of Willie Nelson. As the ironic fate of the Gods would have it, that casino was secretly controlled by the very goons that Bioff had double-crossed. The Mafia's memory runs long, and the lives of those who cross it, don't. On November 5, 1955, Willie Bioff was blown to chunks in front of his wife as he started his pickup truck.

*

"All organizations are born with principles and humanitarian goals, but in their midst the opportunists are never missing and will try to make a profit."

Although Mafia peacemaker Nicola "Uncle Cola" Gentile was specifically referring to the noble origins of the Mafia, his comment had then, as it does today, wide ranging implications in the world of legitimate business (1930s).

*

"Smart money doesn't go to the suburbs. You and your family will stick out like a sore thumb and the feds will always know exactly where you are."

Murray "The Camel" Humphreys gave Mafia Boss Joe Accardo some sound real estate, business and legal advice all in one shot (1950s).

*

"Along with the drugs has come more money but also more greed, more violence, and less honour… Gone are the men of honour whose word you believed in."

Tommasso Buscetta, a high level Sicilian Mafioso turned informant, was reflecting on the good old days when murderers, racketeers, and extortionists did their job with a sense of pride, honour and integrity. He was testifying before the U.S. Senate Permanent Subcommittee on Investigations.

*

"I have killed no man that in the first place didn't deserve killing by the standards of our way of life."

When Mickey Cohen was being interviewed by TV journalist Mike Wallace, Mickey tried to explain that true Mafiosi operated under a strict code of conduct (see previous). Cohen, who was at constant odds with top LA mobster Jack Dragna, was himself targeted for assassination at least four times. Cohen escaped being dynamited twice, blasted at close range by shotgun fire another time, and once in Keystone Cop fashion, saved his own skin by bending over to check out a scratch on his new Caddy just as a bullet aimed for his skull whizzed by.

*

"What has he ever done besides sell olive oil and insurance? Them guys in San Francisco and San Jose wouldn't last two minutes if some real workers move in and take over both towns. Knock over a couple of guys, scare the rest shitless."

Jimmy "The Weasel" Fratianno knew how easy it would be to take over and consolidate the California mob operations. The Los Angeles outfit, while being headed by the inept Jack Dragna in the 1940s and 50s, was such a bush league enterprise that it was often referred to as the Mickey Mouse Mafia by its eastern rivals. Dragna was never really able to control the Vegas operations, making them easy prey for takeover by various New York and Chicago crime families. In fact, Dragna was so inept that when Meyer Lansky offered him a cut in the action at the Flamingo Hotel for a mere $125,000, Jack declined for lack of scratch.

*

"That Constance has the balls of a man."

An unidentified Mafioso commented on Connie, the unforgiving and irrationally jealous wife of mob capo and New Jersey extortionist Philip Rastelli. When Connie discovered that Phil had cheated on her, even after she had warned him to stop, she confronted him in the street and shot him twice. When he recovered, he thought it was safe to leave her, only to have her go to the authorities and start talking even though she was threatened by mob goons to clam up. She continued, and in 1962, the goons' threats became reality and Connie was blasted to death.

*

"The streets will run red with blood, Joey."

This is what a feigning Carmella Gallo cried as she threw herself over the coffin of her assassinated brother, Joseph "Crazy Joe" Gallo. Within five weeks of Joey's death, the blood of twenty seven people killed gangland style, including a number of innocent by-standers, was flowing in New York's gutters (April, 1972).

*

"It would not be the first time a man went to his death because of a woman, nor will it be the last."

The charmed words of bootleg queen Bessie Perri (1920s).

*

"You yellow bellied bastard. You are the lowest and biggest coward I have had the misfortune to meet."

Ann Coppola suffered the eternal pains of purgatory as the wife of Trigger Mike Coppola. On their honeymoon, Trigger Mike used Ann as target practice to entertain his friends. Later on, he discovered the pleasures of abortions and enjoyed watching and assisting on the four performed on his wife, once while she was on the kitchen table. He also beat her, sold drugs to her daughter, and when she filed for divorce, had his thugs beat her senseless. She rebounded and testified in a tax indictment against Mike, for which he served one year. In 1962, Ann committed suicide in Rome by washing down an overdose of drugs with scotch.

*

"Senator, I'm the best goddamn lay in the world!"

Under grueling questioning by New Hampshire Senator Charles W. Toby during the Kefauver Commission hearings, the cool and haughty Virginia Hill made it no secret why she was the top undercover companion for many of the Mafia's big guns. Virginia was born into an Alabama family of ten children, a drunkard father and a grim future. But things quickly changed when Capone's homely bookkeeper Joe Epstein met her. He immediately fell in love and charmed the alluring Hill with wads of cash and tales of underworld intrigue. Convinced, she joined him and over time became acquainted with many of the underworld's bosses, and soon became the mob's trusted "bag lady," transporting huge sums of money world wide. A smart moll, she quickly moved into the beds of other top Mafiosi, including Tony Accardo, Frank Nitti, Joe Adonis, Frank Costello, Murray "The Camel" Humphreys, the Fischetti brothers and her final true love "Bugsy" Siegel. Virginia enjoyed the high life, but after Siegel's assassination, her role diminished. Bored, despondent and longing for the intrigue of the underworld she once knew, Virginia committed suicide in Salzburg Austria in 1966.

Sources

Nash, Robert Jay. *World Encyclopedia of Organized Crime.* New York, N.Y.: DaCapo Press, 1993.

Sifakis, Carl. *The Mafia Encyclopedia.* New York, N.Y. Fact on File, Inc., 1987

Gage, Nicolas. *The Mafia USA.* Chicago, Ill. Playboy Press, 1972.

Messick, Hank and Burt Goldblatt. *The Mobs and the Mafia.* New York, N.Y. Ballantine Books N.Y., 1972.

Mobilio, Albert. *Made Men of Letters.* Harper's Magazine, New York, N.Y., October 1998.

Printed in April 2000 by

VEILLEUX
ON DEMAND PRINTING INC.

in Longueuil, Quebec